# Asylum Bound

by

## Stuart Townsend RMN

Edited

by

Bill Lay

First published May 2012 by P&B Publishing

www.asylumboundthebook.com

ISBN: 978-0-9572789-0-5

## Dedication

This book is dedicated to the staff and patients of "St. Paul's" who had
to live with my childish enthusiasm, yet taught me so much.

# CONTENTS

## ACKNOWLEDGMENTS

MY THANKS GO TO ROGER FOR HIS MEMORIES, SIMON AND SAM FOR THEIR DESIGN AND I.T. SKILLS, BILL FOR HIS COPYEDITING, ROY AND BARBARA FOR THEIR CLINICAL PROOF-READING, TONY FOR HIS BUSINESS ACUMEN AND RUTH FOR HER SENSE. ALSO THANKS TO KAREN AND BEN FOR THEIR PATIENCE IN LISTENING TO THE STORIES SO OFTEN.

# CHAPTER ONE

"God. Has it come to this?"

I still hear this statement as if it was said ten minutes ago. It was actually said thirty-five years ago, in the late 1970s. It was a sentence that could not have been better phrased. Those six words encapsulated everything I was to discover in my psychiatric nurse training. Those words still sit on my conscience. They were the last meaningful words of a condemned woman.

............................

Progressing slowly down the long corridor a social worker led a white haired lady on her arm. Grace had come from a small local village to be admitted to Ward 7. I was to do the admission, my first.

Grace had been quite tall in her prime but now she stooped. In the past she'd probably moved confidently, head held high. Now she shuffled. In her early eighties she retained the echoes of her youthful beauty. Like Lauren Bacall she could still turn heads. Her long white hair shone. I suspected that until recently it had been worn high to accentuate her elegance, her grace. Now it cascaded around her head and shoulders, obviously washed for the occasion although not "set". As I approached a smile lit her lined face; the drab corridor seemed to brighten. She was always thrilled to meet new people and, now that she was in mid stage dementia, everyone she met was new.

When new patients arrived with just a social worker, rather than their family, it felt as though something vital was missing. The place was daunting enough without having to undertake this long walk with a comparative stranger.

I sat with them in the office, open on one side to keep an eye on the day room, the three of us crammed into an impossibly small space, getting her details, jotting down her medication, counting her money for delivery to the administration office and gleaning what details of her life I could from the social worker. Grace sat quietly, just watching. She had lived in a nearby village raising her family. Once her husband had died, just a few months previously, the pressure on the family had grown and, without her husband to shelter her, she had declined quite rapidly.

As problems had mounted the family had contacted social services, which had arranged for admission to St. Paul's Hospital. The family was too busy to provide 24 hour a day care, so the inevitable had occurred.

As I scribbled in her new file Grace perched uncomfortably on an inappropriate upright swivel chair. Her eyes searched hopefully for signs of old acquaintances. As she searched I scribbled, trying to get the flavour of her life into a standard buff coloured file. A standard buff coloured life was the result.

I gently touched her forearm to gain her attention.

"Would you like me to call you Grace?"

"They all call me Grace." She peered quizzically at me. After a pause she asked, "I'm sorry, but do I know you?"

"My name's Stuart, I'm a nurse here. You're coming to stay here for a while. I'll be making sure you're safe and well," I replied, knowing that my job was to see to it that her inevitable passing would be a pain free, if not a "well", experience. I could make her relatively safe, but well? I couldn't promise this miracle.

"Where is this?" asked Grace, staring through the door to the day room, seeing the lines of chairs with elderly people sitting in silence mostly, apart from a sporadic grunt or shout. For Grace there seemed to be no one she knew, but then Grace was unsure if she actually knew anybody. She looked to me for answers.

"This is St Paul's Hospital."

As I watched her eyes filled with tears, which began to run down her cheeks. The smile had gone. I had just ruined what was for Grace a rather odd day out, on the arm of someone who perhaps she knew, to a place that had initially looked interesting. My pronouncement was, to her, a terrible death sentence.

"God. Has it come to this?"

It was said with such pathos that we all fell silent. I had just given her the worst news she could ever imagine. This was more than a death sentence; it was a death sentence in an asylum that she had grown up fearing, hearing rumours about and being warned of by her parents:…. "If you don't behave…..!" St. Paul's Hospital was the embodiment of evil in bricks and mortar. It was the nightmare her parents had warned her of, the nightmare that she, in turn, had passed on to her own children. The nightmare had become reality. The dementia might be advanced but the phrase 'St. Paul's Hospital' would have been ingrained on her grey cells.

3

The inevitable outcome was ignominy and death, a disgrace to her family.

Grace died a couple of months later. During this time she stopped eating. The lovely smile I'd seen on that first day rarely reappeared. She accelerated into a decline that couldn't be stopped. Occasionally she asked where she was. By now we replied that it was an old peoples home, but the deed was done, the cat was out of the bag. The care on Ward 7 might be good, but it was too late. Grace, a mother and grandmother, a respected person in her little community, a tower of strength to family and friends alike, died in my "care".

In her mind she was in an institution far worse than a debtors' prison. Grace, through my carelessness at the mention of St. Paul's Hospital, knew the legacy she left her children. It was the legacy of a mad woman, dying in the county lunatic asylum. Her parents' grim warnings had come horribly true.

Thirty-five years later I am still saddened that, in one of my earliest interactions with a patient, I so casually bestowed on her this most dreadful legacy.

# CHAPTER TWO

I blame the shoes.

Small things can lead to big changes. I was at a major crossroads in my life. Which of these roads to take? Where did they lead? What lay in wait for me? What surprises were waiting round the next corner? It was the beginning of a mystery tour, a mystery tour that lasted over thirty years and only reluctantly gave up its secrets.

..................................................

The interview was coming to an end.

"We've asked you lots of questions. Do you have any for us?" Having failed to receive any satisfactory responses from me they must have been wishing for the session to end.

As usual I was unprepared for this staple question. It was always asked, but at that stage of life I was never prepared for it. Unprepared, it had been the story of my life so far. Lowering my eyes for a brief moment to think up some clever, but not overly clever, question, I saw to my horror a pool of fluid at my feet. Unfortunately, as I had looked down, so had they, following my eyes, and they too saw the same little puddle. It made my blood run cold. Should I start to explain, or would any attempted explanation make it worse? Ignore it, I thought.

..................................................

The year was 1978 and I was a student at Cardiff University; naive, young, lacking in any real experience after four years of bumping along at the bottom of the academic range, due to finish in June. It didn't seem as if theology was going to be of much use in the world of work. Counting how many angels could be balanced on a pinhead or having a grasp of third century church doctrine was of little use when it came to the job market. The interviewers must have been pretty desperate to consider me, but work in the care sector was not overly sought after.

Someone, I don't remember who, suggested that nurse training might be an interesting way to move into paid work. I had no better idea. Although I was devoid of any knowledge of nursing, I did seem to recollect being told that there were many more women than men in the profession and that, as many of the men were rather more interested in their own sex, the opportunities of finding willing women appeared higher than in most other professions. All in all this seemed like a logical enticement to the nursing profession.

So, with this limited but juvenile and sexist perspective, I had approached the Anglia Hospital to start my general nurse training. In my naivety I had assumed that there was only one gateway into nursing, hence the random application and subsequent interview. Unfortunately the interview was in February and, as I left the railway station for the trudge up the hill to the hospital, the snow was coming down. So began the problem of the shoes.

. . . . . . . . . . . . . . . . . . . . . . . . . . . . . . . . . .

These shoes only came out for "best". "Best" meant "most outwardly presentable", perhaps a pointer to the condition of my other pair of shoes. The heels had been quite high; well, I'd always wanted to be a few inches taller, but the heel pads had

6

now fallen off, leaving two not insignificant holes. It was into these holes that the snow had compacted and turned to ice. These underfoot transformations never entered my mind as I sat opposite two nurse tutors in a warm room in the main building. The chair I sat on was high with a forward tilt. It was probably an old chair used for the elderly, to encourage an easier way to rise.

To them it must have looked as though the interview had been just too much.

"When could I start?"

There was a significant pause. Did they really want a young man with both limited knowledge and limited continence starting his general nursing training with them?

"It wouldn't be until a year next September."

This was no good to me: I was jobless, penniless and generally worthless from June.

"I'd have liked to start this September." I pleaded.

There was an even longer pause. "Ever thought about becoming a psychiatric nurse?" they hedged. "They've got places for this September and they're always looking for new student nurses."

The "always" should have been the clue……

I scrambled for a response, brain going into overdrive. My only spattering of psychiatry was what I had gleaned from "One Flew Over The Cuckoo's Nest". Nurse Ratched. Was she to be my role model?

"That would be great! Who do I see?"

The tutors were already on their feet bringing the interview to an end. "Here's the address. We'll phone them now; you can be interviewed within the hour." I was being turned towards the door. "The School of Nursing for St. Paul's is on the other side of the city. Thank you so much for attending."

Two handshakes later, the puddle still obvious, I was ushered out. I suspect that my apparent incontinence would have been a tale to be told to the other tutors for a long time to come.

...............................

The interview at St. Paul's School of Nursing was a mere formality. It was unusual for anyone to actually apply for a student mental health nurse position. Anyone straight from University was almost unique. At the end of the interview, at which, again, I must have given no indication of any useful knowledge, I was asked if I wished to move into the Nurses Home for the foreseeable future. What a silly question!

Signed, sealed, delivered; I was to start in September 1978.

I had signed myself up for a stretch, lasting more than three years, about which I knew absolutely nothing. I was entering a world as alien to me as landing in Australia was for Captain Cook. However, like Cook and his crew, I wouldn't realise until later that my voyage of discovery would be quite so illuminating, albeit with only a fraction of the danger.

But at least I could extend my overdraft on the active promise of a real job.

# CHAPTER THREE

The St. Paul's Hospital Sports and Social Club had a chequered history, very chequered. A committee made up of staff members ran the club, but the secretary and treasurer held carte blanche over the finances. The secret route to making money from the Social Club was a well-trodden path: become the secretary, link closely to the treasurer, run the club, resign as secretary. Lastly, leave the Committee having to work out where all the money had gone. This "sport" was replayed time and time again. Indeed, it seemed to be the only "Sport" remaining that justified the club's long title.

Club members and the asylum authorities had come to the club's rescue many times as successive officials had emptied the tills. When I started the previous secretary had, it became apparent, sold every piece of equipment, including chain saws, sanding machines and cement mixers. All these had disappeared following his brilliant idea of buying, and then renting out machinery for the club. When questions were asked regarding the whereabouts of the machinery, his answer was: "It's out on loan." The machinery was never returned. It was not entirely coincidental that, at the same time, he moved to a new house with much repair work to undertake, and the financial books disappeared, never to be seen again. The finances of the Social Club were a regular pecuniary disaster for the asylum, but a goldmine for the secretary and treasurer.

Bankrupt the Social Club might have been, in a financial sense, but for a new student nurse there was no sense of bankruptcy.

There was a rich vein of interest and information. It would be my Rosetta Stone, the key to my understanding of life in the asylum.

.................................

The sixty-bed Nurses Home had stood for perhaps a hundred years or more. Behind it was a grass tennis court, unmarked, the net long gone, the grass rarely cut. No one played there any more, although one staff member would tell me that he could recall the French nurses who, in the past, had sometimes played topless. He admitted that, as a youngster, he'd often crept on all fours to a safe vantage point from where he could relish such voluptuous displays of flesh.

The French were the earliest remembered of the immigrants to work in the asylum. It was always a place where recruitment was difficult. The Filipinos and the Spanish, who settled in groups to work at St. Paul's, followed the French. Recruitment from these countries depended on the advertising work of the chief male and female nurses, who would trip off to these far away climes to drum up unsuspecting staff. The promise of streets paved with gold, could never match the reality. When they arrived, St. Paul's Nurses Home and its environment could only be something of a disappointment, as my arrival had been for me.

The Nurses Home was a fine manor house about a mile from the asylum, with a sweeping staircase and large bedrooms. An annex had been attached during the 1960s in modern brick, and it was here that I moved into a small room with a bed, washbasin and desk. Length of tenure led to the better rooms in the old building. As I lived there for more than four years I eventually progressed to the largest room overlooking the tennis court. This progression in status was mirrored in the asylum, where some well-behaved patients progressed from a dormitory to a single room with a few "home comforts". But sadly, for many patients, it was more of a decline towards a bed by the office window where they would die, overlooked by the staff.

Having unpacked I was bored. My chattels were few. I wandered through to the TV lounge in the old building. A frumpy woman in a dressing gown sat watching "Coronation Street". She didn't even look up.

"Hi. I've just moved in. Where is everyone? What do people do around here?"

Annoyed at my interruption, she was terse. However the adverts had started, so she deigned momentarily to focus on me. "Only about thirty of us live here. Most stay in their rooms or go out with friends. But there's a staff bar at the hospital. The Social Club. Round the back. Usually someone there."

She turned back to the TV, conversation over. The adverts had finished. 'Corrie' was back on.

I don't do loneliness well, being naturally gregarious, so sitting in a room with this frumpy woman watching 'Corrie' was the last thing I wanted to do. I felt that much of what I needed to learn could be picked up through meeting staff. Apart from actually working, this would be the best way of gathering the information required for my new role of student nurse, about which I was totally ignorant. In time I came to realise that this information gathering was the second most important purpose of the Social Club, after cheap alcohol. I got on my bike.

...........................

The Social Club was behind the hospital, beneath the rear of the theatre/recreation hall. With few windows it was entered down steep steps. I got to know these steps well. The outside toilets were at the top of these steps. Navigating them after a heavy evening was no easy task. The handrails were loose and the steps were chipped. The toilets regularly overflowed, so the steps held rancid puddles for the unwary. Inebriated staff were regularly found in a heap at the bottom of the steps from where they were rescued and returned to their bar stools. A dank and stale smell pervaded the area. It was a mix a stale cigarettes, stale beer and overflowing toilets. Empty barrels and other paraphernalia cluttered the entrance, the stairs, the toilets, even under the fire escape, Although the whole place should have been condemned on health and safety grounds, it was my type of place. I grew to love it.

Twenty years later it was closed forever. Thirty-five years later I returned. I found that the clutter remains, odd empty barrels, cigarette boxes. Locked gates prevented any entry. It also prevented any need for clearing up.

Despite its lack of fixtures, fittings and embellishments, most of which had been flogged off by the previous secretary, it was still the essential place to finish a shift with friends, as well as a source of invaluable information about new experiences in the world of the asylum.

Inside there was a bar to the right, a few chairs and tables to the left and a fruit machine and space invaders game. One person was playing the fruit machine, a stack of coins balanced precariously on top. Five people sat at one end of the bar chatting quietly. One sat at the other end, filling in a crossword. No one sat on the chairs with tables. Indeed, in my experience, no one ever sat there. A small group in a darkened archway leading to the TV lounge chatted loudly and drank heavily. A TV blared next door, but no one was watching. People turned at my entry, then returned to their activities, ignoring me. I was entering into their world. Strangers could be a threat.

"A pint of bitter please," I asked the bar steward, a name badge informing me of his rank. Middle aged, he had a beer belly showing dedication to his work, but he showed no smile and not the least bit of interest. I found out later that although he was the full-time bar steward, his wife and daughter both worked in the hospital - hence his job. He stared at me in silence. He made no attempt to get me a pint.

"Do you work here?" He asked, turning away, pretending to tidy.

"As of tomorrow. That's when I start," I said rather proudly, expecting, if not a free drink, then at least a hearty welcome. Neither was forthcoming.

"Are you a member of the St. Paul's Sports and Social Club? You can't drink here unless you are." He started to refill an empty glass for one of the gang of five at the bar.

"Do I need to be, for tonight?"

"Yes. And you'll need to be proposed and seconded before going before the committee for approval. OK?"

It was probably easier to become a member of the Knights of the Order of the Garter....

"O.K. But can I have a drink now?"

"Not unless you're signed in as a guest." Well, they did give him the title "bar steward". Perhaps there'd been a spelling mistake. The less than helpful "bar-steward" was giving nothing away. No help, No clues. So no pint. He moved to the far end of the bar and sat on a stool. Conversation over.

"Can anyone sign me in?" I raised my voice for him to hear at a distance. I was not giving up.

"Only if they're a member."

I suppose my need to meet people was more than a need. It was a compulsion. If it hadn't been I would have left. The steward was paid with a nightly wage, not as a percentage of bar-takings. He was just there to serve, the fewer the customers, the easier the night. I'm sure he knew that the previous bar steward had been the one to blow the whistle on the previous club secretary after weeks of unpaid wages. He probably expected the same thing to happen to him one day. With this to look forward to he was a very grumpy "bar steward".

A prop forward of a man, eighteen stone at least, with a bruiser look, but the first smile I'd seen, saw me struggling. He broke away from the far group and came to my rescue with a hand outstretched.

"Hi. I'm Ray. I'll sign you in. I'm a paid up member," he said warmly.

"I'm Stuart. Thanks. Just moved into the Nurses Home, but there's no one around and I'm gasping for a pint. A woman told me that this is where to meet people."

"..... Where the important people are," he said emphatically.

An ex-policeman and ex-rugby player Ray was now a nursing assistant. He would, in time, qualify as a registered nurse. I bought Ray a pint (he was never an expert at buying pints for others; still a skill to be learned). He asked what I knew of the hospital but quickly moved to talking of his experiences. He was in many ways old school, although he'd only been working in psychiatry for a year or so. He was taken on primarily because he could "handle himself". If a problem kicked off then a phone call would go round the wards for help. The statement "I've got Ray on my ward," would lead to an inward cheer. He was a one-man flying squad. "Send him over now." Problem sorted.

I propped up the bar, buying the majority of the drinks. We chatted till closing time.

"What's the School of Nursing like?" I enquired.

"Bunch of tosspots. Not been near a patient for years. Nurse teachers and tutors are just failed nurses. They know nothing. …Just create trouble, think they know it all, but fucking crap when there's a problem that needs sorting." He leaned back, twisting his neck to address the man behind, engrossed with the crossword. "Isn't that true Jack?"

Jack didn't look up but Ray wasn't going to let him get on with his crossword. He shouted again. "I say, Jack! Isn't that true?"

Jack turned his head to Ray, but not his chair, or his body. He wanted peace, not discussion. "Yeah." He turned back and filled in a word, or at least looked as if he filled in a word. Perhaps he just wanted to make the point that he didn't want to join in. He was content to sit quietly doing the crossword and leave Ray to show off to this new student nurse.

Ray, quite unperturbed and quite oblivious to Jack's brush off, continued at great length about the useless tosspots of the School of Nursing, as well as the rough and tumble of life in the asylum. "Tell you what, you don't want to go near such and such. He'll deck you soon as look at you." Ray had not just climbed on his high horse. He was positively galloping.

By the end of the evening, when the bar steward ejected us, I had listened to his interminable monologue of violence and struggle, whilst paying for a disproportionate number of drinks. St. Paul's was clearly a place in which only the strong survived. We were the last to leave, apart from Jack who folded his newspaper and politely open the door for us as we left.

Although Ray had a lot to say, by the time I returned to the Nurses Home I pictured the asylum as a cross between Bedlam and Cardiff City Centre on a Saturday night, but without the police. Life here was going to be tough.

# CHAPTER FOUR

Mrs. Eaton was now very old; her husband had long since passed away. When I met her at a minor social function in the city, she was interested that I was a student nurse at the hospital where she had spent so much of her life. Dr and Mrs. Eaton had lived in the house that all previous medical superintendents had inhabited. It still stands, but in 1960 it was situated just beyond the walls that ringed the hospital. Her husband, Dr Eaton, was "the old school of the old school". Dressed in an immaculate white coat he would, once a week, do his routine rounds, always ending with a shrug of his shoulders, letting the white coat drop untidily to the floor as he walked away. The charge nurse from the last ward was expected to pick it up and send it for cleaning.

It was at this function that I was introduced to this lady who had been the wife of the medical superintendent at the hospital during the period when the walls had come down.

A path led from the hospital, through a locked gate in the wall, to this large house. Mrs. Eaton described the day the wall had been breached, the gate unlocked, allowing free movement between the hospital and their house. I expected a story of her conversion to the joys of freedom, to the rights of the patients, to liberty.

Standing tall, with a matching twin-set outfit, her hair in a tidy bun, Mrs. Eaton folded her arms over her ample bosom and peered down her nose at me. "Never forget, young man, that it was my husband who initiated the removal of the wall. As I've said to so many people, I still consider that he's not had proper recognition for the sweeping changes he made." She failed to mention that he didn't, in my eyes, do this from some form of altruism, but rather because a new law insisted on it.

"I remember the actual day it occurred." I was now hearing history as it had happened. "That morning the wall was removed from the section near us. I was in the lounge. My maid informed me that three patients from Ward 2 had wandered over and were standing outside the front door asking if they could have a cup of tea. She didn't know what to do."

I could see where this was all going. She would say that she had instructed the maid to give them a cup of tea.... And that they had been very happy... And that she was so pleased that they at last had their freedom to wander. This was what I expected.

However:..... "I told the maid to inform the patients," she announced regally, "that she would make a cup of tea, but that as she was waiting for the kettle to boil, with the patients waiting outside for the expected free beverage, that she should phone Ward 2, get a few burly nurses to come over and instruct the nurses to bundle them back to the ward immediately. They did, without any bother at all."

Mrs. Eaton moved on. She had taught this young student nurse a thing or two. There was history and there was HER history. Walls can be removed, but it takes longer to change attitudes. The walls may have come down but this powerful matriarch of the hospital wanted the old social order maintained, walls or no walls.

So what was it like? The Hospital was one of a type, lifted from the top shelf, sealed in a plain wrapper, labelled "Only for the Very Disturbed".

The typical mental asylums were built within about twenty years of each other in the late Victorian period. Once you know one, you can pretty well walk round any, being mostly designed to a stock in trade template. Same shape, same water tower, same wandering people, same sense of hopelessness.

A traffic roundabout welcomes you. Directly in front is the main building where the Queen might be dropped off if unfortunate enough to make a royal visit, which, of course, she never would. To left and right, a ring road, ringing the asylum itself. The road winds round the outside of the wall, though the wall has long gone leaving just the road. To the left female wards. To the right, male wards. A tall water tower dominates.

The main building, quite striking unlike the others, has three floors. The ground floor is for reception and administration. The first floor is where the medical superintendent and chief nurse had their offices, overlooking everything that came through the front door. The top floor is for patient and staff records, pokey rooms full to bursting with brown files collecting dust. This main building, visible from the road, is the only concession to any attempt at style. Behind this building everything is functional, solid but dull. A central corridor runs to left and right. Any attempt at style has disappeared. The building is now plain brick with no embellishments. This corridor housed the inner wards. This corridor was where the action was.

The corridor that linked the inside wards was always known for its extreme length, the bigger the hospital, the longer the corridor. In the huge London asylums the corridors stretched forever. Now lino floored (they used to be parquet) they were still buffed daily by the cleaners with electrical polishing machines. The wards, dormitories and day areas were wrapped around this main artery. Although the wards were "home" to patients, in reality they were poorly designed warehousing units and a common thoroughfare to the other wards and departments. Most of the wards lay along that echoing corridor. There were advantages and disadvantages in this. Having part of your home as a pedestrian precinct, open to all, can cause both interest and friction.

The older long stay patients would pitch their chairs in this corridor to watch the passing crowds, much as they would have done on Blackpool promenade. Just as the deckchair syndicates would collapse their chairs at night, so the charge nurses tried to discourage this motley collection of tatty armchairs cluttering up the corridor, by moving them back to the day rooms at the end of the shift. But they always reappeared at the crack of dawn, ready again for the morning sittings. Floor-standing ashtrays accompanied these easy chairs. Interaction between patients on a ward was minimal. Interaction between patients on differing wards was virtually non-existent. Like meerkats each ward would defend its manor. Patients from any other ward were distinctly unwelcome. Yet nomadic patients would run the risk of possible attack in their desperate search through the ashtrays for discarded cigarette ends. Of course, the resident patients of any ward had already scoured their own ashtrays but one dub-end was still worth the risk. Any dubious prize had probably been smoked at least twice already, but it was added to the awful second, or perhaps third, hand remains of other dub-ends, gathered in a bag for rolling or trading later.

The passing trade of people through the wards was the highlight of an otherwise boring day for the patients. It was an opportunity to scrounge fags from unsuspecting travellers, verbally abusing those who didn't cough up. The corridor also served as a catwalk for the female patients, an opportunity to strut their stuff in front of male patients, who might be prepared to pay a small fee for very dubious sexual favours.

In time I, like all "asylum staff" driving around any unknown town or city, could spot the asylum. They had a look that screamed, "**Bin your unwanted here**." Although many have been converted into luxury apartments, with neatly mown lawns, beautiful flowerbeds and mature trees, to me they still scream "asylum!"

Opened in the late 1800s, St. Paul's Hospital in its heyday was "home" to around 1500 patients. It had the smell and feel of a monastery. Here was a semi-self-sufficient community, bound together by a series of rules but with little or no contact with the outside world. It was in the community, but not of the community.

Even though patient numbers dropped from the 1960s onwards, this didn't mean a reduction in new infrastructures, quite the opposite. There was no stopping the spread of the buildings around the periphery. New heads of department needed visible demonstrations of their prestige; the NHS always seemed willing to give them these symbols. A new Head of Psychology? "We'll build you a new Psychology Department." Psychiatrists, like almost all consultants, then and now, demanded beds. Never mind whether they were filled, the number of beds for consultants denoted the size of their empire. A sparsely populated empire held the same rank as a crowded one. A contagion of new buildings would spread to service fewer and fewer patients, but at ever greater costs.

Somewhat bizarrely, on my return to the place in 2012, still open, the buildings had spread even further, though the total patient population of the old asylum building is now no more than forty. Unlike most asylums this one hasn't been sold, probably owing to the fact that the "authorities", in their wisdom, have built a new medium security forensic unit right next to it, thereby ensuring that the asylum can't be sold. Who'd want a potential Hannibal Lecter beyond the fence of their well manicured back garden!

By 1978, although the building continued, the patients had been drifting away for at least fifteen years; a residue of about 450 remained. Some of the central wards stood empty or had been roughly converted to "day facilities". Outside, where vegetables would once have been grown in plots, all such horticultural industry had ceased, the patients left being unable, or unwilling, to tend them. No one took responsibility for the chaotic rambling roses – all leaf and no flower.

This was no longer a walled or prison like environment. Unlike the walls of so many old cities, there were no remnants of the large wall that had completely surrounded St. Paul's Hospital. Did the wall keep patients in, or society out? I never knew. Removed in 1960 to indicate the newly enlightened image of the hospital, the fact was that this hospital, like all others, was now subject to the new 1959 Mental Health Act. This Act completely altered the situation of the patients, no longer inmates, no longer lunatics but supposedly normal citizens, with rights of their own. The "new" Mental Health Act changed the emphasis of mental ill-health. The focus moved from the rights of a community to incarcerate it's unwanted, to the rights of the individual patients to know why they were placed in such a dread place, and how they could extricate themselves from it. It was a real change for the better.

Asylum should imply a retreat, a place of calm away from the hustle and bustle of life. The term "asylum" comes from the Greek word "asylia", special religious areas where slaves, debtors and wrongdoers could seek sanctuary, free from arrest by the authorities. As early as 490 AD there was a hospital in Jerusalem devoted to the mentally ill. In 872 a similar institution opened in Cairo, but both were mere drops in the ocean for the vast population they had to serve. During the middle ages a variety of settings were used to "house" the small proportion of the mentally ill deemed "mad" enough to warrant locking away, monasteries being the most popular choice.

In England in 1217 a priory for the sisters and brethren of The Order of the Star of Bethlehem opened in Bishopsgate in the City of London (on the site of what is now Liverpool Street Station). It became a hospital in 1337 admitting some mentally ill patients. It did not become a dedicated psychiatric hospital until later, named Bethlem.

Bethlem, or "Bedlam", became notorious. Conditions were dreadful; care amounting to little more than restraint. Violent and dangerous inmates were manacled or chained to the floor or the wall. Bedlam became a byword for the brutal treatment of the mentally ill. In 1675 this "hospital" moved to new buildings in Moorfields, beyond the City walls, but its reputation lived on. The playwright Nathaniel Lee, his mind allegedly "unhinged", was incarcerated in Bedlam for five years from 1684. He was not best pleased: "They called me mad and I called them mad. They outvoted me." He recovered, only to die in a drunken fit in 1692.

Inmates of Bethlem were first called "patients" in 1700. "Curable" and "Incurable" wards were opened for public viewing, becoming popular attractions and drawing gawping visitors from afar. For a penny you could stare into their cells, view the "freaks" and their antics. For cheapskates entry was free on the first Tuesday of each month. In 1814 there were 96,000 visitors. But things were changing. In 1815 Bedlam was moved again to St Georges Field, Southwark. In June 1816 Thomas Munro, Principal Physician, resigned as the result of scandal, accused of "wanting in humanity" towards his patients. A new enlightenment? Perhaps.

In stark contrast to the callous brutality of Bedlam, the York Retreat opened in 1796 in the countryside outside York. It was developed from the English Quaker Community both as a reaction to the harsh, inhumane treatment in other asylums of that era and as a model for Quaker therapeutic beliefs. A common belief at the time was that "the mad" were wild beasts. So recommended treatments included debilitating purges, blistering, long-term restraint by manacles and total immersion in cold baths, all administered in a terrifying climate of fear and brutality, as at Bedlam.

Quakers maintained that the humanity and inner light of a person could never be extinguished. When one of their congregation, Hannah Mills, died a few weeks after being admitted to the local asylum they investigated. The asylum had not allowed friends or family to visit. The Quakers found that inmates were treated worse than animals.

The Quaker, William Tuke was enlisted to take charge of the project, the new "Retreat". Despite the contemporary views on "madness and insanity" Tuke was a strong believer in the importance of benevolence and a comfortable living environment. When the Retreat opened in 1796 there were no chains, no manacles and physical punishments were banned. Treatment was based on kindness and care, restoring the self-esteem and self-control of patients. Early examples of Occupational Therapy were introduced: walks, farm labouring, and gardening. Patients could wear their own clothes and wander freely in the grounds. The Retreat became, and remains, an asylum in the true sense.

However, though the York Retreat was a beacon of enlightenment, from the early 1800s new, harsher and more traditional asylums grew in size and number, from a few dozen "inmates" to hundreds. In 1800 there were, perhaps, a few thousand "lunatics" locked in a variety of asylums; by 1900 the figure had grown to a hundred thousand. This growth was directly proportional to the development of "the Alienists" (so called because they dealt with people who were "alien" to society). Alienists were the precursors to psychiatrists.

As the Asylums turned into huge overcrowded custodial institutions, so restraint again became the method to control the burgeoning numbers. The over-population of the asylums continued until the 1960s.

Although the term asylum was changed to "Hospital" during this period, in reality asylum was a term still used by staff to indicate its history. It was built as an asylum. It looked like an asylum. It was a lunatic asylum. No change of name made any difference.

Before 1960 (when the new Act was implemented) most of the asylums in Britain were subject to a range of antiquated laws. The Lunacy Acts and the County Asylums Act, of the 1840s, together gave asylums the authority to detain "lunatics, idiots and persons of unsound mind". These laws provided for the safety and security of the community, allowing people to be incarcerated for very long periods (often their entire lives) without any real recourse or appeal for freedom. They were there to keep the community safe. The troublesome or difficult patients were regimented and worked in order to keep them "out of mischief".

The walls enclosed not just the buildings of the asylum but the potential dreams and aspirations of the patients. It was only in 1959 that the Mental Health Act superseded the Lunacy Act of 1890, the change from "lunacy" to "mental" perhaps the verbal indicator for much more than just the dismantling of the wall.

Before the 1959 Mental Health Act a person entering the hospital would be allocated to a work detail and expected to graft for long periods to "occupy" them. So a lad of 20, perhaps a vagrant or petty thief or just a social misfit, could be placed in St. Paul's, put to work on the "pig detail" and, if he was good at his job and the pigs were fattening and profitable, would have even less chance of being discharged from the asylum. The pigs needed him, so the asylum needed him. The medical superintendent would be less than happy for him to take his newly acquired skills elsewhere. After all, who would look after the pigs? A successful apprenticeship in the asylum never opened doors, never led anywhere, just to tending more pigs; indeed, a whole lifetime of tending pigs.

A woman in her late teens, perhaps with an unhappy childhood or having a child outside marriage, could quite easily be placed in the asylum by parents or guardians, and from there be sent to the work detail of sewing or darning, to keep the "fabric" of the asylum going, so to speak. On admission she might get a diagnosis of "Indolence" or "Immorality". The asylum would not be wanting her released either. She saved money by repairing the sheets, tablecloths and dresses. The embroidery and needlework would be something for the hospital authorities to show off, displayed at Summer Fetes and the like. It never seemed odd to show off the painstaking work done by these asylum seamstresses. No one ever seemed to ask, "If they can do this, surely they could be properly employed, trained and normally housed?"

In time most "inmates" would settle down to become compliant, resigned to their lot in life. The community of the asylum would ensure its low running costs and the continuation of the semi-self-sufficient system of order inside its walls. Top grade patients would provide manpower not just to the asylum, but also to the senior staff, providing free labour for personal gardening, building, painting and even car washing for the medical superintendent and chief male nurse. The very best patients, the elite of the asylum, would be "rented out" to farmers to clear their fields or get in the harvest. Where the profits went was never discussed. One thing was certain; the patients never received a Christmas bonus.

By 1978 many patients had received the additional diagnosis of "institutional psychosis", so discharge became even more difficult. I remember two patients receiving an engraved medal, at a special ceremony, from the area nursing officer for sixty-five years of "service". They were, sadly, delighted. They should have sued. Where are lawyers when they're needed?

Within weeks of starting at St. Paul's Hospital I was looking after these two patients, who had admission dates of 1911 and 1916, with bizarre admission diagnoses such as "intellectual insanity" or "masturbation insanity", patients who had lived all their adult lives in this walled, locked community and had never known any difference. Although the walls had gone, these long stay patients were thought beyond release. Their present diagnoses were almost as ridiculous, "probable mental impairment", or "personality disorder with schizophrenic symptoms". In truth they had been there so long that no one was sure whether they were mad, whether the place had made them mad, or whether they were sane, but now settled! But without them, what would the staff do?

Staff in many of the asylums joined the same unions as prison officers, although at St. Paul's most of them joined public sector unions such as CoHSE or NUPE. Few staff would consider joining the Royal College of Nursing (R.C.N.), which was seen both as female orientated and timid.

Many staff came from families that had always worked in the asylums. Groups of staff with the same surname continued the traditions handed down to them. Both of my best friends, who had started as student nurses in the early 1960s, had parents who'd worked in the hospital. It was as traditional to continue this family vocation, as it would be for sons to follow their miner fathers to the pit face. Following in a father's footsteps didn't guarantee any preferential treatment. One older staff member told me, "I never had preferential treatment from Dad. But there was once when he told me to empty the pockets of a patient, who'd been collecting the rubbish he'd found while on the farm group detail. I was trying to get the patient to part with his precious garbage when he took a swing at me. Dad floored him before the second blow. That was the only time he got involved."

Those who trained prior to 1970 would not have worked anywhere in General Hospitals and were far too tribal to consider a joint qualification. The R.M.N. qualification (Registered Mental Nurse) was the "macho badge". The S.R.N./R.G.N. (State Registered Nurse/Registered General Nurse) was for "the girls". Occasionally, for male student nurses, the S.R.N. badge was a short course after an R.M.N. qualification, but only if you'd already bedded all the available female nurses at the asylum and needed a change!

So young sons and daughters provided ongoing care to those their parents had cared for before them. They would already know the "old lags" of the asylum, having been "shown" them on the sidelines of the football field or in the theatre. They would have been educated in all the tricks and ploys needed to survive. They had grown up with asylum counterpanes with SP woven through the design lining the dog's basket or on the back seat of the car. They had met the odd and the aggressive patient, being taught by parents how to address them. Children of asylum staff knew about "odd" and generally accepted it. They would have grown up hearing the stories over the dinner table. Staff grew up and grew old with the patients. Their tolerance of "odd" was remarkable. The staff were much more amused by the foibles of other staff than the foibles of the patients. Patients did as they always did; staff were far more unpredictable.

These staff members were able to live much of their social lives within the asylum, with tennis courts, football field, cricket field, staff bar and restaurant, bowling green and theatre. It was all there. Why pay top prices elsewhere when the asylum had it all? But when I started, the tennis courts were growing weeds, the nets were gone, the bowling green was reverting to meadow, the football field was still there but the goals were bent and rusty. The cricket pavilion had lost its windows and the wicket, once one of the best in the region, was as unkempt as the rest of the outfield. Round the pitch random pieces of machinery, the huge rollers and side stands once neatly paraded in top order, had become weird central structures around which wild plants grew. The theatre was rarely used, a huge hall and stage echoing to times past, its only use now was as a shortcut from the nursing administration office to the Social Club, for "early orders", removing the inconvenience of going outside.

By 1978 the community of the asylum was in its death throes. Those patients who could move out, had moved out, often just going home, no longer plagued by the voices. The asylum, like other enclosed and separate communities before and since, was coughing up blood as intake declined to almost nothing. Its lingering decline was long and distressing. It was death by a thousand cuts.

Acute units for short term psychiatric care were moving out of the range of the asylum, either to the General Hospitals or to stand alone units. The wards remaining were the long stay, mostly VERY long stay, and the elderly. When "the elderly" were sold off to the private sector, the end had come. I joined in 1978 and watched the asylum in terminal status. The asylum in its death throes was an exciting and compelling school of learning for an inquisitive student nurse.

Those who worked those last years of the asylum are left with feelings of ambivalence. On the one hand there were aspects of the institution that are sadly lacking today. However, most of us recognised that it was a fundamentally flawed and, at times, abusive institution.

Staff at St. Paul's looked after each other, as large disturbed families do. This protection was exemplified when a charge nurse on a long stay ward having spent too long in the Social Club, staggered back along the corridor and sat drunkenly at his desk. He opened the top drawer, removed a bottle of scotch and polished it off. Standing to go, his legs buckled beneath him. Somehow, using the desk as a prop, he dragged himself upright and stumbled towards the door, intending to drive home. At this point a number of older charge nurses arrived, warned of the impending danger by the existing staff.

Unable to reason with him, they removed his keys and offered to take him home themselves. The old charge nurse wasn't having his authority undermined by anybody and threatened anyone who restricted his freedom, lashing out at staff who dared oppose him. The only solution was to grab him, put him in a side room, lock the door and wait till the morning. Quickly, with the least force necessary, the charge nurse found himself incarcerated, locked in a side room of his own ward.

By the morning he had sobered up, but in the meantime he had destroyed the locked room, smashing everything that could be broken in his frustration. When confronted by management about the damage to the room, staff all agreed that the destruction could be put down to a particularly aggressive patient, a Ukrainian. This was accepted by the powers that be. The Ukrainian could speak no English. Who could argue?

The asylum system was my starter to a main course of thirty plus years in all the major areas of psychiatry. It remains the most memorable experience of my working life. The friends I made there have remained my friends, even when I was living as far away as New Zealand. A funeral for a staff member still draws the same crowd, looking rather older and frailer, but the stories are re-shared, amidst raucous laughter.

The community of the asylum still cares for its own.

# CHAPTER FIVE

Betty, the first tutor to give us a lecture, was on her last lap before retirement. Eight weeks later she was gone, to live out her days, free from the demands of the asylum. With smart but dull, indeed rather dowdy clothes, she appeared quite upper-middle class, yet her voice had a strong Cockney twang to it. That first lecture was on safety. There weren't many lectures that held my attention. This one did.

She described her first day in the asylum where she'd cut her teeth. Betty and another student nurse were sent to the locked rooms in a North London asylum sometime in the late 1930s. They had been instructed quite clearly to "stick together". On arrival a nurse took Betty to the first locked cell. The student nurse with her, so she said, had made a few comments about trusting to one's instincts and not being frightened, so went further up the corridor. At the end of the shift the student nurse was nowhere to be seen. A search followed and, at last, she was found under the mattress of one of the patients. She'd been strangled.

The lesson was: "Stick together. Take advice. Accept that if someone tells you that a particular patient is dangerous, it is best to believe them!" After my late night session in the Social Club here were yet more warnings of danger and violence. I was good with neither. Why hadn't I waited for general nurse training where patients lavish nurses with presents just for being "nice"? Or was this just another of my misconceived youthful fantasies?

The St. Paul's School of Nursing was a far cry from academia; cobbled together, a mixture of "portacabins" and prefabricated buildings making a sorry sight. Staff who were in the front line of mental illness, especially for those on the wards, the school was usually held in disdain. "Failed nurses" was how nursing tutors were viewed. There was little common ground between the School and the asylum. It was not just the self-congratulatory obsession with the theoretical that annoyed the ward staff, it was also the interference and potential threat the school posed. Student nurses were welcome on the wards as long as they went along with the charge nurse's views and ethics. Indeed, charge nurses would actively check out which students might present "trouble". Troublesome student nurses? All the fault of new-fangled ideas instilled by the School of Nursing. It was seen as part of the charge nurses' job description to bring uppity student nurses back to earth with a bump.

Sixteen student nurses started in my group in September. By the end of the training, there were only four, the rest having abandoned the course for one reason or another. One middle-aged woman, naively accepted by the School of Nursing, lasted only 4 days. Her Jehovah's Witness background suggested to her that mental illness was somehow connected to God's displeasure, God's punishment. Although St. Paul's was outdated, it wasn't going to return to those days, reflecting on hundreds of years of this religious bigotry.

We met each day in the School of Nursing, a prefabricated building next to another weed-ridden tennis court. Four tutors and a head tutor gave us the grounding we needed. Or so they fondly believed.

In our second week we were split into small groups and sent to various wards to be assessed on feeding and shaving a patient. It was to be the first test of my competence. We were all thrilled to be doing something practical at last. I was actually setting foot in the hospital. My adrenaline was pumping. My excitement was childlike. I knew absolutely nothing about nursing and not much more about illness.

I had been brought up in a family that was mercifully free from obsessive concerns about health. Visiting the Doctor was a last resort, Mum usually sorting out the problem with little or no fuss. The wider family was even less concerned with medical involvement, thus leaving me somewhat bereft of knowledge about the more personal functions of the body. Indeed it was one of the standing jokes of our family when we heard that an aunt of mine had spoken quietly to her husband of a problem she had been literally sitting on for some weeks. She told him that she was suffering from "I.B." and didn't know what to do about it. When first told this story, perhaps when I was old enough to cope with it I presume, I had no idea what I.B. was. Some terrible disease? No. It was the family acronym for "itchy bum".

My uncle suggested that as it had been going on for some weeks, it might be best for her to go to her local doctor. The thought was too horrific for my aunt to contemplate; hers was a male doctor! After some time she approached my uncle again and pleaded with him to go to the doctors instead of her, telling the doctor that he had the I.B., that he should get some medicine and pass it on to her. The pressure on my uncle became too much and he at last visited the GP, telling him with huge embarrassment that he had been suffering from I.B. for some time. Would he therefore prescribe something for it? He was mortified when the doctor asked to examine the offending orifice. "No sign of any problems there," the doctor confidently diagnosed, uncle pulling up his trousers. My uncle duly protested that, although signs were invisible, could he still be prescribed some cream. The doctor agreed. The cream was conveyed in turn to a rather shamefaced aunt.

So, as my grasp of bodily functions and procedures was probably even more limited than others, a visit to the sick ward had a real sense of entering a whole new world.

Walking into the asylum for the first time, along that long corridor, was overwhelming. People wandered in so many different ways up and down the corridor, at speeds so differing that I couldn't help but watch and wonder. Some hurried, with staccato steps. What was their rush? Where had they got to go? Some walked normally, at least what I thought of as normally. I assumed they were staff but was uncertain. Some strode, but so slowly, almost in slow motion. Some shuffled quickly taking tiny paces. Some just stood still, staring. At what, I couldn't tell. There were no windows or notice boards to study. For the most part some just seemed to stare at a blank wall. Why? Orderlies buffed the floor with whirling machines, careful not to interfere. This chaotic ballet fascinated me, but I had to keep an eye on the tutor who was striding ahead.

I followed, eyes everywhere, everything was so new, so different. There was a full-sized billiard table to the right in a room that looked like a large conservatory. It was monopolised by staff, or at least men wearing white coats. White coats were, at this stage, the only visual clue for a naïve student nurse as to who was who. Staring goggle-eyed at this brave new world I failed to notice that the student nurse in front of me had stopped. I stumbled into her and gave a red-faced apology. "Don't worry," she replied. "It's all so weird, isn't it?"

Our little band of novices had stopped. "Hi Jack," Ben greeted a chap I recognised. "Not seen you for ages. Where're you working now?"

I knew where I'd seen him. Down the Social Club. "Hello Ben. Still skiving in the School of Nursing are you?" A little dig I was sure. Ben didn't take the bait. "On 7s now. Been there six months. Taking my mate Percy to the General Office to deposit his money. No time to chat." Jack glanced at the student nurses, eyeing two women who were pretty. Then he saw me. "Hi there. Didn't catch your name but saw you down the Club, with Ray. Sorry not to be more sociable. Didn't really want to join in. Ray can be a bit of a bore."

"I'm Stuart. Nice to meet you. Expect I'll see you there again, sometime. Got a lot of info from Ray, but not really sure how useful it'll be. Finish your crossword?"

"Nah. Five left. Saw the answers today. Made no sense."

He pointed at a small man standing alongside him who I'd failed to notice. "This is Percy. Percy, meet Stuart." Percy wandered on, eyes down, obviously other things on his mind. Richard turned and smiled. "There! Now you've met one of those dangerous patients Ray told you about!" He giggled. Then he and Percy were gone.

Commonly known as "The Sick Ward", Ward 14 was primarily for those in other wards who were severely physically sick. On Ward 14 they were either nursed back to relative health before returning to their own ward, or they died. Either way there was quite a rapid turnaround of patients. The workings of Ward 14 were as alien to me as a meeting of the Hellfire Club would have been to Margaret Thatcher.

Ward 14 was a Nightingale ward – beds lined up eight in a row, with tatty curtains separating them, like something out of a "Carry On" film. With twenty patients, two qualified and two unqualified staff during the day, the staffing level was higher than other wards. Sister Beechy (in those days sisters were women and charge nurses were men but both were the same rank) of Ward 14 was a full-blooded traditionalist: frilly hat, frilly arm cuffs, belt with a fancy silver buckle, and the very image of "Carry On Matron". She prided herself on being very much of the old school, still checking that the wheels of the beds were all strictly facing the same way and that the pillowcases always opened away from the entrance to the ward. She was quick to point out these details to anyone who'd listen. It was her raison d'etre. No one cared.

Sister Beechy had recently moved to Ward 14 from the acute wards. The traditions she'd upheld had been of no use in the challenging environment of the acute situation. In addition, her communication skills left much to be desired. The crunch had come when she had decided to sit down, in a small office, with a patient who'd all too regularly thumped other patients. Sister Beechy felt she could alter the mindset of this volatile patient with some words of wisdom. "Look, I know how difficult it must be for you, how frustrating life is. When you feel that you're at breaking point and want to hit a fellow patient, go instead to a member of staff."

In hindsight the outcome was obvious. The jaw and nose healed quickly, but it was considered that a move to a geriatric ward would be best for everyone concerned.

Her whole being now reflected the traditional nature of the care provided on this ward. Her patients received good basic care, not always an easy task, as I was soon to discover. Woe betide anyone who failed to give her patients enough to eat or drink, or failed to clean and wash her patients to her high standards. Charge nurses were generally still all powerful. "The basics" is what the charge nurses did and "the basics" were what they were proud of. Sister Beechy could do "the basics" with the best of them.

Marion, a staff nurse, welcomed me. I had briefly met her down the club. She could guzzle whisky with the best of them. She told me she was into threesomes.....! She took me through to the dining area.

The type of chair a patient sat in, defined the patient. Chairs that were around tables were taken by patients who were getting better, or at least not getting worse. These patients only needed direction and reminders. Chairs with trays that slid in and out of the arms contained patients who were restless and wandering. A butterfly screw on either side, thereby totally trapping the patient, once in place, would secure the tray. There was no way out. Easy chairs, fully reclining, were for the very poorly, small bundles of humanity cocooned in blankets, pillows, rugs and towels; little wizened faces gazing out without focus. Often a staff member sat on the arm of the chair, gently touching the incumbent.

Three particular ladies who suffered from dementia sat in these low chairs and it was decided that I would feed one of them. The noise level was high, what with staff trying to pass on information, the TV in the corner blaring, various shouts, screams and swearing from patients round the tables and the clatter of spoons on plates.

I was given a plate of mashed up food with instructions that two glasses of squash would also be needed by the lady I was to feed. I had never seen food that appeared so unappetising, but at least it was genuine food rather than many of the processed foods now given. I realised very quickly that this task was an art form that required great skill.

The lady I was feeding would jerk arms and legs with no regularity, lacking any focus at all on what I was trying to do. The eyes didn't follow the spoon. The mouth didn't open when the spoon approached, but only when the spoon actually touched the lips. There was no warning of the thrashing limbs. They could be steady for a short while, and then one, or maybe all four, limbs would jerk suddenly. Time and again a random limb would connect with the spoon, throwing the contents onto the floor, the wall, my clothes, or others nearby. Sometimes the spoon reached its destination, but often this would happen at the same time as an involuntary shout. My tentative offerings would again be rejected.

After an hour I was sporting a fair amount of food, as was the floor. However, overall, the lady had received a small meal and two drinks from a mug with a spout.

But what struck me most of all was that, in all that time, I had only fed one lady. The other two ladies had a much better service from the staff that had fed them. Their immediate surrounds were significantly less decorated with gobbets of semi-digested food.

A clinical teacher, sitting in to judge the competencies of the student nurses, informed me that I was "satisfactory" in feeding a patient. Satisfactory perhaps summed up my attempt. She wanted to know how I'd done with the shaving part of the assessment. I had spent all my time feeding and hadn't shaved anyone. It turned out that the other Students had already shaved the male patients on the ward. There was no one left to shave. Yet the clinical teacher couldn't pass me unless I had actually demonstrated my ability to carry out this personal procedure. She arranged to come back with me another day. Some poor soul would have the experience of a shave from me, which would probably result in razor gashes worse than their original five o'clock shadow. It would be a toss up between stubble and facial lacerations.

As we were about to leave there was a whispered conversation between the clinical teacher and Sister Beechy.

"You can ask him, if you want to," I heard her say.

"A gentleman died about an hour ago. He'll need laying out. If you'd like to help with this, he will need a shave. This could be your assessment. You don't have to, of course, but it would sort out the problem."

Although I had no comprehension of what the term "laying out" meant, I was undeterred. I was beginning to understand what a different world this was. Everything was completely, amazingly, thrillingly new to me. "Of course." I said.

The curtains were closed around one bed in the ward. Marion, the staff nurse, took me in. A wheeled trolley was next to the bed, which was covered with a blue hospital counterpane, the outline of a man lying underneath. My heartbeat increased as she lowered the counterpane to reveal the top half of the deceased man. He had been perhaps 70, of a dark complexion and certainly very stubbly. I'd never seen a corpse before and was apprehensive about how I'd cope. Two impressions hit me. One was the colour of the man, the greyness, the peculiar sense that he was a man, and yet not a man. One eye was still partially open, the other fully open, which worried me. Would he blink? My other concern was the feeling that although there could be no doubt that he was dead and even I could see that he'd been dead for some time, I had this disturbing feeling that at any moment he might sit up, speak, move. He was dead, but would he come back to life?

Marion asked if I was feeling all right and, reassured that I was not about to pass out, took me for the first time through the procedure known as "last offices".

The counterpane was completely removed and a towel spread over his genitals. I was shown how to mix up soap to create a lather, and how to stretch each area of the face to allow for a close shave. I was constantly worried that I'd snag him and that he'd shout, "Watch what you're doing, for God's sake!" Gradually I grew in confidence. I got closer and closer, turning the face, stretching each fold. I was aware, after a while, that I was talking to the corpse, telling him what I was doing, apologising if a scrape was not quite right. At last I finished. I washed his face for one last time and stepped back to have a better look. I decided that, apart from the open mouth and still unevenly opened eyes, the face looked pretty good.

We turned him onto his side. His back and buttocks were mottled and blue. Blood, I learnt later, sinks to the lowest point of the body after death, hence the mottled appearance. As we turned him various gurgles and rumbles occurred which startled me. Marion was already washing his back. Using forceps she packed his anus with cotton wool balls before turning him again. Taking a thin bandage she passed it to me. "What do you want me to do with this?" I asked, already having an inkling of what was needed.

"He needs that tied round his penis so that it doesn't leak urine. Just do it tightly and tie it off."

Despite feeling distinctly queasy, I did as I was told. What I was doing would surely tell me if he was still alive. Lastly she packed his throat with more cotton wool balls and put two damp gauze swabs over his eyes to shut them. His dentures were fetched and I put them in. He had lost weight during his decline, so the top set no longer fitted snugly. They went in, but as the jaw slackened, the teeth dropped from the roof of his mouth. "Leave that," said Marion. A toe tag was attached to his big toe with his name and date of birth. A pillow was put under his chin, closing his mouth and pushing the dentures back into place. Marion lifted his right hand. On the forefinger was a small gold ring, which she covered with a piece of sticky plaster.

"Why are you covering that?" I asked.

"To make sure no one helps themselves to it and that it doesn't fall off. The family say he's to be buried wearing it, so that should make sure it stays with him."

"Who'd take it off him?" I asked.

"The undertakers. But not the ones his family has chosen. They're pretty straight."

"So do most people keep their rings and get buried or cremated with them?" I wondered. Always the questions.

"Depends. Many of the families take them back so that they can be passed on through the generations. But some families just want them for cash. Indeed, a family only the other week insisted that I go over to the mortuary and get the false teeth out from a corpse as they'd heard they could sell the second hand dentures for fifty pence." There was nothing I could say to this. Families are complex things.

Lastly a sheet was wrapped round him. All finished. Marion then made her only negative comment. "We do all this, but the undertakers will charge the relatives for last offices, even though we've already done it. Why should they get paid for what we've already done?"

I was unsure at that stage whether to feel satisfied or to feel that I had intruded. Yet this task had been done with respect and professionalism and I had been a small part of that. Marion led me back to the Clinical Teacher. I had passed my first practical exam. I felt that I had not let myself down. It was certainly a VERY different world that I had joined.

The difference between the practicality of the asylum work and my judgement of the irrelevance of theological work led me to make a simple decision on that first shift. I would never return to theology, in any form.

Yet when I look back now on that first shift in the asylum, after all these years, I realise I had fallen into the mistake that I am most critical of in others. I had carried out the Last Offices procedure knowing nothing about the person or the relatives behind the corpse. So when I think about it now, there is no link to a man, a father, a worker, a person. It was a corpse, without a history. A nobody.

# CHAPTER SIX

Wimbledon it was not, but fiercely competitive matches with Jack, Bob and others, helped open many doors in the asylum.

Starting and finishing shifts were constant sources of frustration for management. They had tried various methods of ensuring staff started and finished at the correct times, but had given up. They were well beaten on every occasion. Signing in was attempted after the Union had adamantly refused a clocking on system. This "signing in" became a game for charge nurses and older staff, a game to win – a game to enjoy. Single bicycle pedals or broken bicycle chains were collected and kept in a plastic bag, to be used as an excuse for late attendance. "Don't come here complaining I'm late. I went straight to the ward rather than wasting time trying to find the nursing officer. You can see that the sodding pedal dropped of my bike on the way..." they'd insist, holding the pedal as hard evidence. Nursing officers chasing a charge nurse, already on the third round of drinks in the Social Club, would always be told that they were "just on another ward, liaising". A further phone call would find that the elusive charge nurse had "just left". It was a futile chase without a visible quarry. The system looked after its own. Nursing officers were not part of this system. The nursing officers never went in the Social Club, just as the Queen never went to the House of Commons. They weren't members. They weren't welcome. They weren't there.

That evening I returned to the Social Club. I had arranged to meet Ray. Between him and another staff member I joined, paying my dues. The bar steward reminded me that I wasn't a voting member until the committee, at the next Committee Meeting, had approved my application, but as the Club still had debts to pay from the last secretary, the chance of me being black balled was slight.

My day's experience on Ward 14, and my first encounter with a corpse, was recounted with huge pride. On reflection I suspect that my youthful excitement would have been a source of wry amusement to the staff propping up the bar, for whom such stories were just old hat.

Just after seven o'clock the bar started to fill. Male staff always wore the uniform, a grey suit, with a white coat to wear on the wards. I was aware that most of the men sitting on the high stools at the bar were still wearing these suits. They were technically still on duty. More staff arrived, forming new groups. The older men, charge nurses, all seemed to be holding court. Each seemed to have a pint of bitter with a large scotch alongside. They were chasing, a phrase I became very familiar with. "Pint and four fingers please," they'd ask. Mostly they had doubles, though some would have two doubles alongside their pint. One of them asked me if I'd like a pint; I gladly accepted. I was shocked when I returned the favour, finding myself buying four single scotches for his chaser!

What I hadn't grasped was that this was the handover time for many of the wards. The night staff were coming on and the day staff would be off at eight forty-five. The old lags, the senior charge nurses, would only work till about seven o'clock, the earliest they could drop off their day report. It would be scribbled out at ten to seven. At five to seven they would casually wander down to the Nursing Office, behind the hospital theatre, conveniently close to the Social Club. They hoped the nursing officer wouldn't ask any difficult questions. The report deposited, they would slope quietly off through the theatre to the Social Club, where the serious drinking would begin. They were always there until at least a quarter to nine, their official finish time, so technically they were available. If needed they could be called back to their wards, but realistically it would need to be a pretty drastic crisis. They would have already left the ward keys in the top drawer of the desk for the night staff. Night staff wouldn't usually bother with a verbal handover; they just read the day report. A word of mouth hand-over required a visit to the Social Club.

One man was perched at the corner of the bar, with his pint and chaser. He introduced himself. Bald, short and chubby, he smoked a small cigar. He had an impish grin that was welcoming.

"Hi. I'm Bob," he said, shaking my hand. "I gather you've just started. How's it going?" A middle aged woman in a nurse's uniform, with a badge telling us she was a staff nurse, sat alongside him. I couldn't help noticing that every so often he would stroke her leg or rub himself against her provocatively. Bob, like the others, was having his handover.

"Wonderful," I replied, "or perhaps I should say weird."

"You'll get used to it. By the way, do you play tennis?"

Desperate to be a part of this brave new world I was quick to respond that I played, but not well.

"Join us on Saturday morning for a game … all very friendly …. We'll go to the pub after." This short conversation altered my life.

So, that Saturday morning there were four of us, Jack, the crossword solver who I'd now met twice before, Bob, Linda and myself. Bob was no longer in the prime of youth, being small, potbellied and balding. He was a charge nurse on one of the elderly wards. He had come up through the ranks, often waiting for a more senior position by way of dead men's shoes. He told me that on the day he had had his interview for his first charge nurse post he had slaved away learning the various parts of the Mental Health Act and appropriate management responses to a variety of problems. With this quickly mugged up knowledge he was quietly confident of success. However, when he had turned up for the interview, the chief male nurse started by saying: "Sell me a vacuum cleaner!" He felt that his impromptu stab at this had been quite effective and that, perhaps, if they had asked more about nursing, he might not have been successful.

He always had a smile, a smile that would change to a glint when he was with women. He was known for being something of a Lothario having chat up lines that just seemed to work. He later said that his knack lay in never pretending to be anything other than a joker. Women would fall for this, initially thinking he was harmless; they soon learnt better. He had this off to a fine art.

Bob, despite his shape, as well as his drinking and smoking addictions, was a natural sportsman, had played football to a reasonable level. He saw everything as a challenge. Cryptic crosswords were his main activity on a Sunday morning on early shift. He would work tirelessly until the crossword was completed.

He and I usually played together. We were a team, though we each blamed the other for points lost. On the other side of the net were Jack and Linda. Jack was only slightly younger than Bob but had started at the asylum before him. Although married to a Spanish woman, a sister on the wards, their relationship was rocky, disintegrating during my time as a student nurse. Jack and Bob were regular partners in tennis and cryptic crosswords. Taller, with a beard as well as a permed haircut, Jack was a charge nurse on another elderly ward. He still played football for the hospital team, which regularly caused shift problems on a Saturday. Jack, like all the rest, loved working weekends. Doctors doing their rounds didn't bother them and, more importantly, they were on double-time. But Jack also played football, every Saturday, leaving his ward rather understaffed. Taking time "off" was never on the cards. "You scratch my back" was his motto. At St. Paul's Hospital, back scratching was contagious.

And then there was Linda. In her final year of training, she was a stunning young woman who always wore clothes which made the opposition drool. Whichever side of the net you were, the views were spectacular. Serving, when Linda was your doubles partner, was never easy. Crouching, frilly-knickered, in front of you, made it impossible to watch the ball; I lost many a match through double-faults. Returning serve, when she was your opponent at the net, was quite perilous.

Bob and Jack were very aggressive in their play, they never held back! Bob was the only player with any sort of subtlety, with a spin to his shots which none of us could replicate. Jack and I both aimed at the person at the net, intending to take them out the hard way. Usually, if they could get out of the way, the ball would still be climbing when it hit the back netting. But the speed of return meant that it was both difficult to get out of the way as well, as a huge temptation to respond to the challenge by smashing the ball back, straight at the sender.

After the match we retired to a pub, an excuse for a game of darts and a few pints. A tennis match always ended with all the players going home "tired and emotional".

As time went on these tennis matches became even more competitive, with more people attending. The tennis was far from elegant but, God, was it fierce. As the days shortened it was decided that we really should try to continue through the winter. This led us to join the local Sports Centre where they had an indoor tennis court. Unfortunately the building had been originally designed for three badminton courts. The tennis court had been crammed into this restricted space, leaving a gap of just four feet between the serving line and the back wall. It was a wooden floor, the bounce was very long. The players had to volley almost everything. Long rallies didn't occur, just speed of light shots which one either avoided, one was battered with, or one fluked a return. A full smash, landing at the back of the court, would ricochet against the back wall to hit you on the back of the head.

I became known as "the chap who called out" to a ball even before the ball had landed, in the belief that if it was close to the line, then it was probably out. Despite the terribly competitive edge to the games, and you'd be reminded for ages if you lost the last game, or had played a wild shot, I never remember any bad blood. At the end of a rally, usually very short, it would culminate in all four players collapsing in heaps of laughter. The only disputed calls were mine, but they never held this against me

These tennis matches allowed me to meet most of the staff that would influence me. What I never worked out was if this was for the good or the ill of my career. It certainly meant that as I moved from ward to ward, I was already known.

This, in turn, led to me being accepted faster than other Student Nurses.

"Oh, Stuart's alright. He's a mate of Jack and Bob."

Wimbledon it certainly wasn't. But it did open doors.

# CHAPTER SEVEN

It took only one shift for me to realise that the so-called preparation given in the School of Nursing was in fact no preparation for the experience of life on a long stay ward.

As my first shift on Ward 2 wore on, more and more patients paced the corridor. All I could do was watch. They walked from the top of the corridor to the office and then back, repeatedly. At times they stopped, fixed, rigid, often at the top of the corridor, with their heads turned into the corner, like the old fashioned school dunce, but one who had been forgotten and left there. They remained motionless. Some bent forward slightly, to rest their heads, shifting their balance. One always leant against the door of the corridor leading to the rest of the hospital, his brow pressed to the reinforced smoked glass. The imprint of the stippled glass would remain on his forehead after he moved. If you happened to open the door he would fall towards you, suddenly awake, or alert. Gathering himself up he would utter a few threats, then shuffle off, up and back, only to reach that exact same position against the door on his return. This little interlude would last about fifteen minutes and then, for no reason obvious to me, he would regain an upright position, turn, stare, and start the routine again. It went on all day, every day.

I wondered what was going on. What were these people doing? What was my role? What would my involvement be? As time passed I had more and more questions, but most went unanswered. The people – the patients – were so irretrievably damaged. There would be little I, or anyone else, could do for them.

Even now I don't know how much my reaction to, and fear of, some of these patients was due to their outward appearance. Here were patients with seemingly untreatable psychotic illnesses, living permanently with their disturbing delusions and hallucinations. As if that wasn't bad enough, they were dressed in clothes fit only for a hobo, not necessarily old, but spotted with cigarette burns and spilt food. On top of that were the side effects of their medication: the staring eyes, the protruding tongues, and the angry jaws. To crown it all, a haircut from hell. Their handicaps, many actually created by the asylum, were innumerable. How would I cope? More importantly, how did they cope?

When we had started at the School of Nursing we had been given, along with our suit, white coat and passkey, a timetable containing all the details of where we would be working for the next three years or more. It was rather disturbing to see one's life mapped out for such a long period. For each experience there would be two weeks of preparation in the school. These two weeks were felt to be ample. In reality the two weeks were interminable. Having had a taste of the novelty and excitement of the wards, the last thing we wanted was to sit behind a desk and be lectured to.

Ward 2 was at one end of the long corridor so there was no passing trade through to other wards. This meant it was refreshingly free of stained chairs. No chairs meant no ashtrays. No ashtrays meant no raiders. It was a nest of, and not a recipient of, raiders.  Side rooms lined the long corridor. These were the secure cells of the old days with heavy prison doors. Walking down the corridor I could see beds made up with the St. Paul's Hospital counterpanes but little else. The rooms were featureless, a bed, a washbasin and a chair. There were no personal extras giving any indication of individuality or character.

Downstairs were the day areas, upstairs the main dormitory. About thirty men, aged 35-80, lived their lives to a rigid daily routine. This fixed routine, once probably so restrictive to new patients, had become the framework around which their daily activities were planned.

It was exactly 1.15 pm when I stepped into the office for my first shift. Behind the desk sat a smallish, round woman in her 30s, June, a staff nurse. To her left sat a wiry, Bryllcreemed, black-haired Irishman, Niall, the charge nurse. Thin as a rake, with the demeanour of a compere at a sleazy nightclub, he was a boss with a chequered history. With absolutely no fear of management he ran the ward to his own set of rules. It was time for "handover". In theory, this was a period of overlap between two shifts when professionals could update each other on the business of the day. This is what I'd learned in the School of Nursing. The memory of that first handover was what it didn't do; it certainly didn't tell me anything about Ward 2 or the patients. Ward 2 handovers were about social arrangements. I soon assumed this was the norm.

June was taking over for the afternoon shift. Niall was finishing, having just got back from the Social Club, and wanted to get off as soon as possible. His own pub was waiting for him. June introduced herself and Niall, before moaning about how she had to see the doctor because she had a chest pain. Without so much as a blink, Niall stood up, reached over, slid his hand down the front of June's uniform under the bra and fondled her breast for a few seconds, before pulling out his hand and saying, "can't feel any problem with that." Not a blink from anyone. "Anyway, there's the handover," he said, pointing to the Day Report. "Any problems, don't contact me as I'll be in the pub." With that he was gone. Was this how handovers worked, I wondered? It was somewhat different from the descriptions given by the Tutors in the School. How odd.

June showed me round the ward.

"How many patients are there?" I asked, seeing only a handful.

"Thirty, when they're here" she replied, walking up the corridor, pointing at single side rooms without comment. Empty of patients, they were devoid of personality. The walls were painted in asylum white, the counterpanes were all "St. Paul's Blue", with "SP" woven into the corners. The beds were tubular black iron. The bedside locker contained just one item, a Gideon's Bible, not a tradable commodity so it was just left there. Anything else would have been snatched and traded. The TV was blaring in the communal lounge. Just two patients sat facing it, neither of them actually watching, their eyes focused elsewhere.

"So where are they all?"

June shrugged. "Who knows? They'll be back for tea though. They wouldn't miss that. Let's go and meet Uppa," and she strode off up the corridor.

Hovering in the doorway of one of the side rooms was a man in his mid fifties, wearing very tatty trousers and jacket with the usual alarming institutional haircut.

"This is Uppa. Say hello Uppa."

His mouth stretched and pulled as if he was constantly yawning.

"Uppa, uppa, uppa," he grunted, with a sort of belching noise.

"That's why he's called Uppa," said June, "that's all he says."

"How long's he been here?" I asked.

"For ever. Probably since he was about eighteen. Everyone knows Uppa."

"So, what's wrong with him?"

"Dunno. Could be he's partly subnormal. Could be he's gone like this. But he's great. Aren't you, Uppa?" She patted him fondly on the back. This was the vague inconclusive response I came to expect in answer to any of my questions.

For some, the attainment of the R.M.N. qualification gave them the luxury of not having to ask any further questions, let alone seek answers. They were qualified, they had the badge, they had the increased salary, and so further knowledge was irrelevant.

"Uppa, uppa, uppa."

As Uppa spoke he spat and turned his head in a writhing motion, the mouth movements heavily pronounced, with tongue projecting. He had no known relatives, no next of kin, and his only interaction was with the staff on duty. He didn't go to any of the day facilities, only the top grade qualified for that, so he just stayed, wandering around the ward. Uppa glanced briefly at me, turned and wandered off.

The face and jaw stretching, a condition known as "tardive dyskinesia", was caused by very long usage of anti-psychotic medication. In Ward 2 this disturbing side effect was common to many patients. On the one hand the anti-psychotics had been a boon to people, indeed, a positive revolution. But, on the other hand, they had such appalling side effects. Tardive dyskinesia has no known treatment. Once evident, the damage is done.

The next patient I met was Steven. June pointed to a striding man, "This is Steven." He didn't give me so much as a glance. I was just someone who would be there for a moment in his life, not worth acknowledging. He was tall, slim and perhaps thirty years old. I felt immediately threatened by him. He sported yet another alarming institutional haircut, the shagginess of which suggested it could have been done by a patient in the Occupational Therapy Department. He wore an old sports jacket and trousers. His eyes were staring. As he approached he stopped suddenly. "Fuck off!" he barked to one of the imaginary voices that plagued him. His undirected aggression shook me. He moved on only to repeat this process again and again and again. Rarely still, he strode the ward, up and down the corridor, suddenly poking his head into a room, staring, swearing, and then moving on. He had no communication with others, although the shouting and abuse went on all the time. If he sat it was only for short periods, with his legs kicking out, as if tapping his feet angrily to some savage beat, though there was no music that I could hear. This agitation was, again, due to the side effects of his medicine.

He was wild and frightening. I tried to understand why. I had no feeling of wanting to spend time with Steven. To me he was the incarnation of the beast from a 70s horror movie. I could only wonder at the nature of the monsters that were tormenting him.

"He's alright as long as you don't challenge him," June said unhelpfully.

"So, what challenges him?"

"Anything to do with personal care: changing his clothes, bathing, his injection, anything like that." So, he was fine, so long as there was absolutely no contact whatsoever. Steven was not going to be easy.

I soon learnt that in Ward 2 "long stay" really meant long stay. It was for the totally institutionalised, the damaged goods left over from the old asylum system. Patients on Ward 2 were there for the duration. As time progressed, as my "experience" progressed, I learnt that they could be roughly divided into three groups.

The first were the severely psychotic, suffering from the delusions and hallucinations of a totally untreatable schizophrenia. Steven was part of this group. Medication was still given but there was no sign that it had any beneficial effect on their condition, except to send them to sleep. The anti-psychotic medication provided no relief from their tormenting demons.

The second group, the majority of Ward 2, also suffered from schizophrenia, but with this group the anti-psychotic medication had some beneficial effect, but it was never enough to allow them to return to society. The strength of anti-psychotic medication needed to reduce the delusions and hallucinations led to such disturbing and disabling side effects that further isolation was inevitable. The battle was to find the right balance. Whatever the result of the battle, it was always the patient on the losing side.

The third group was made up of patients who fitted no particular diagnosis, who had been in the hospital for so long that no one was interested anymore in why they were there. They took no medication. Why should they? In all probability they now suffered from institutionalisation to a degree where even a minor change of routine brought on great fear. The asylum itself had reduced them to this, to a reliance on the very institution that had created the problem. Decisions were now beyond them. They expected to be told what to do, where to go, how to behave. Like Uppa, they were there because they had always been there.

Some on Ward 2 were war veterans. Some of these "Vets" were Poles. Unable to return to Poland after the communist take-over at the end of the war, half a dozen talked their way through their auditory hallucinations in Polish. They paced the wards, hunting cigarette ends with the rest, but language problems made them even more isolated from the staff than the English patients. Like all the others they had no verbal contact amongst themselves, just contact with their "voices". Once a week the Polish Society of the city would visit and take them out to the pub. What they did there, how they behaved and what they gained from this I never discovered. The Poles were probably safer in the asylum, at least safer than if they went back to Poland.

Despite being together for upwards of thirty years, in a closed environment, eating, sleeping and living together, there was no significant interaction between patients. They passed each other without acknowledging each other's existence. They knew of each other but without any conversation, consideration or interaction. Despite thirty years of so-called companionship, they remained almost total strangers to each other.

George was tall, well-built and about 40. He walked with an abnormally long stride, rubbing his head most of the time. His head was always bent, always looking at the floor. If he looked up, it was with his eyes only. His head was always down. There were two small scars on the side of his head. I later discovered that these were the scars from a lobotomy. Did the lobotomy make him better or worse? No one ever told me.

He and Steven passed each other many times a day as they paced the corridor. They never spoke to each other, never bumped in to each other and never acknowledged each other's existence. Occasionally Uppa might accidentally blunder into one of them and a fracas would ensue. Uppa would initially "hold his own" though staff would rush to rescue him. But no one else bumped into either of them, for fear of being thumped.

George and Steven lived in complete isolation. Both needed fortnightly injections about which they would be warned the day before, and again in the morning, and again an hour before. No one wanted to tangle with either of them.

Here were thirty men, living in a closed community, like medieval monks, but existing in almost total isolation. Admission conferred on the patients the same primacy of tenure as for the Pope in St Peters. This placement would be where they would die. The closest they would come to interaction with fellow patients would be as dragooned mourners at one of their funerals.

# CHAPTER EIGHT

Bath time, a simple enough procedure, one would think. Who wouldn't enjoy a long soak in a hot bath? Well, Harry for one.

David, the other charge nurse on Ward 2, had a very different approach to Niall. For a start his handovers were more formal than Niall's; there was no breast fondling. The question of Harry's bath kept coming up during each handover. Everyone agreed that it was time for him to have a bath, though no one suggested when it should be, or who should put him in the bath. David kept raising the subject but clearly didn't want to "do the necessary" himself. Neither did anyone else. "He'll need a bath in a few days..." but no one volunteered. A few days came and went. The few days became a week and then a fortnight. June and Niall played for time, but with time progressing, and no bath forthcoming......... They would point to the "Nurses Notes" showing that they had undertaken all the previous baths. It was clearly David's turn to "do the necessary" so they were reluctant to put themselves forward again.

Eventually Niall's nerve snapped. "Well, if no other bastard'll do it, then me and Stuart'd better do it. Be an experience for him, but it pisses me off. Why is it an experience I get again and again and again?" He stared at David who just ignored him. David was on his last lap of clinical work, shortly to move to the School of Nursing as a tutor. What minimal "dirtying of the hands" he'd done was done.

Later that shift Niall took me aside. "Right mate, you'll enjoy this. Follow my lead."

"Why's it such a fuss to get him into the bath?" I asked.

"Could leave him, I suppose. He stinks now; he'll stink more if we leave him. When would you deal with him?" Niall said.

"Couldn't he just have a wash?" I was looking for alternatives.

"Needs more than just a fucking wash. He eats, sleeps and works in those clothes... never takes them off .... no chance of getting them when he's asleep. He needs a bath. His clothes need a wash."

"Why doesn't he wear pyjamas?"

Niall didn't see it as his role to answer naïve questions from Student Nurses who weren't even wet behind the ears.

Questions frustrated him. Anyway, that was what the School of Nursing was for.

"Look," he said, getting visibly agitated, "he's never worn pyjamas. Went through the fucking war in the same clothes. Harry and pyjamas just don't go and it's not going to do any fucking good trying to make him wear them. Harry is Harry. He's been wearing the same clothes for five weeks. They need washing as much as him. Can't leave him in these same clothes forever, can we? It's got to be done. Accept it. Anyway, once he's got his kit off and the bath is ready, he gets in and loves a soak. Spends ages in there. But he won't do it without a scrap."

Harry had been in the hospital since the end of the Second World War. Originally diagnosed with schizophrenia, he now had an additional diagnosis of untreatable tertiary syphilis. Harry was confused and disorientated, but he knew his own territory, the ward. Take him out of the ward and he quickly panicked unless he was with a member of staff he recognised and trusted.

During the war Harry had been in Singapore and had been captured by the Japanese. There followed three years of captivity and terror in the POW Camps. He was one of few to survive. What he saw there scarred him for life. Although a firm favourite with the staff, even coming to their rescue if they were attacked by other patients, he was not safe around anyone with oriental features. His language would coarsen and, given the chance, he'd attack them. To him they were all still the enemy. His dementia caused Harry to confabulate; he would fill in the gaps of his memory by making responses he felt were appropriate, even if they weren't true. Confabulation is sometimes seen as "honest lying" with no intention to deceive. He called all male staff "Master", not as a term of subservience, but as a variation of "Mister". It got round Harry's inability to remember names.

Harry, in a more extreme way than others, was fiercely independent, probably feeling that he was something important in this big building, which, of course, he was. He couldn't care for himself properly although he was too proud to accept personal care from staff.

Small and wiry, with a tab end always hanging from his mouth, Harry could get quickly frustrated. He didn't regularly pace the corridors, but when he did he would sometimes bump into the regulars, especially Steven and George, leading to outbursts of violent language, mostly from Harry, who couldn't understand what these intruders were doing on his patch. He considered all the other patients "mad". Indeed, in some odd way, he thought of himself as a member of staff, but was unsure what his role was, as he didn't quite realise that his home was actually 'the asylum'.

Niall went through to the bathroom and ran the bath, frustrated by my questioning. The bath run, he found a complete change of clothes for Harry, obviously not belonging to Harry, but roughly of his size. This bundle was placed on an old cork stool alongside the bath. He then returned to me.

"Take off your coat and tie. Could be a bit of a battle. The last thing I want is a dead fucking student on my hands," he quipped. "It'll be no worse than a pub fight in Tipperary!" I removed my coat and tie, wishing I had my motorcycle helmet with me, and perhaps a flak jacket. All right, I didn't feel I was entering a war zone, but I knew there was a battle to be won.

I couldn't see how this forced bathing was to be done. We were going to be the ones starting the fight. It felt odd being the perpetrators. Niall walked through to the Day Room. Harry was standing there, tab end hanging in the corner of his mouth.

"Bath time Harry," Niall ordered.

"No. Don't want one Master."

"Yes you do. Come on Harry."

Harry strode past us and up the corridor. He was escaping. I was at a loss.

Niall hurried after him, took his hand and started to move him back towards the bathroom. Harry broke lose and strode off, back into the Day Room. I, as usual, followed behind. This type of confrontation was completely new to me. I was a fish out of water.

"You're having a bath!"

"No I'm not, Master."

"Oh yes you are!" It was turning into a pantomime.

Niall grabbed him by both arms and started to lead him towards the door of the Day Room. Harry went berserk, dropping to the floor, arms flailing and feet kicking. As Niall leant over to lift him, Harry got to his feet and bolted. Niall clung on. Harry dragged himself back into the day room, with Niall clinging onto him, unable to alter the direction, which was now away from the bathroom. Harry reached the sofa at the far end and collapsed into it, now completely intertwined with Niall. They were locked together in a twisted embrace. From underneath, Niall looked to me for help. I had no idea what to do.

"Get his legs!" With that I became just as entangled as the other two. I had his legs. Niall had his arms. Harry was swearing and threatening blue murder.

"Get him up. Let's move him out of the bloody day room!" Easier said than done: Harry was struggling to get away; I was struggling to keep a hold of his legs and Niall was struggling to control his flailing arms, whilst trying to escape from the bottom of the pile. The twisted human mass was struggling desperately, but no one was crossing the gain line. Niall remained stuck underneath, his arms pinning Harry's from behind. Three bodies were stacked like a squirming sandwich, with Niall at the bottom, Harry in the middle and me on top. There was a brief pause. We all gasped for breath.

"Can you smell burning?" squealed Niall. "Christ, I'm on fucking fire!" In the melee Harry's cigarette end had been knocked from his mouth and was now burning a hole in Niall's tailored shirt. Niall slapped frantically at his chest to dowse the glowing ember.

Harry's feet started kicking at anything that he could see. "Jesus, Joseph and Mary! Get his fucking shoes off before he kills someone!" shouted Niall.

I grabbed a flailing foot, steadied the limb and ripped the shoe off, glad to be of some use. "Not MY shoes. HIS fucking shoes, ya' pillock." I looked at the shoe. It was much smarter than Harry would ever wear. In this tangle I couldn't tell one foot from another. Niall was still crushed underneath, unable to move, having gained a hole in his shirt and lost a shoe. He must have been cursing himself for agreeing to show me how to "do the necessary".

Gripping Harry's legs tightly with one arm I finally found his feet and pulled his shoes off, trying to ensure I still had a grasp on his legs. I didn't want to get kicked in the face. In the commotion, the human sandwich had collapsed sideways, allowing Niall to get his feet to the ground. Movement was now possible. Despite the lack of a shoe, Niall and I rose unsteadily and carried Harry down the corridor to the bathroom, arms still flailing and legs still kicking.

Harry managed a last ditch defense by clinging to the doorframe of the bathroom. Niall prised each hand free. More swearing from Harry, but we were almost there. As I held Harry's feet, Niall tried to remove his remaining clothes, but to remove the torn shirt he had to let go of one arm, allowing Harry to land one final blow to my head.

"Just get him in the fucking bath. He'll do the rest!"

We dumped him in the bath still clothed. Harry thrashed the water desperately, drenching us, but he was in. We got out quickly, tired, bruised and wet, but victorious. The door was just ajar. I sneaked a look. Harry was removing the remainder of his clothes as he reclined in the bath, dumping them on the floor in a rank and soggy heap. As I continued to watch he settled and began to sing to himself. When he wasn't looking I crept back into the bathroom and took away the drenched clothes leaving the clean ones for Harry to put on. Harry was lying back relaxing, loving the comfort of a nice hot bath.

An hour later Harry reappeared in the day room, smart and tidy, with a new tab end on the go. For Harry the battle had been forgotten. It had been one hell of a battle just to sort out personal hygiene, but, for the life of me, I couldn't think of any better option. So much of what happened in the asylum had this effect on me. Many things didn't seem to be right, yet sometimes difficult decisions had to be made, and followed through. Life here was not a simple black and white divide. Life in the asylum was grey, in all senses.

Staff didn't exactly queue up to bath Harry. It was always a battle. The usual pattern of battles in the asylum was predictable. Staff always won. But with Harry things were different. One day Harry might win.

# CHAPTER NINE

Chemical restraints were not pleasant. Most asylums had their own particular speciality. Indeed, within each asylum, most charge nurses would have had their own well-tried variation on the in-house cocktail. In St. Paul's it was known as the Black Strap, a foul and legendary concoction much talked about by the old lags. It had been a revolting mixture of a sedative, usually chloral hydrate, mixed with a bowel busting cocktail of laxatives, especially senna. The patient was made to drink a beaker full of this brown ooze before being put into a locked room. He was left, with a commode beside the bed, to "rest". When he woke he wouldn't get much further than the commode owing to the violent effects of the anti-constipation medicine. For the patient it was a brutal, exhausting and weakening experience. Such cocktails were still in use as late as the 1960s. They were an alternative form of restraint, a logical progression from the old-fashioned straightjacket.

The use of restraint in the asylums had been accepted as a consequence of the huge numbers of patients. A new world was opening up to me, previously invisible, which I needed to understand. Where to start? To understand about the asylums, it becomes necessary to understand something about the terrible illness of schizophrenia. The big hospitals had become the sink for many thousands who suffered this appalling affliction.

Schizophrenia, the name given to this dreaded illness, roughly translates as "splitting of the mind". It is an illness recognised the world over, the delusions and hallucinations, the withdrawal and apathy, the thought disintegration. For centuries these terrible torments had been seen and known but not treated. There was no treatment. People just had to suffer.

Symptoms of schizophrenia are commonly defined as "positive" and "negative", the positive implying "extra" to the norm and negative, "less than" the norm. Positive symptoms, the "extra" symptoms, are the hallucinations and delusions. Negative symptoms include lethargy, withdrawal from society, tiredness and apathy.

Although hallucinations can be of all five senses, they are most commonly experienced as "voices". To the sufferer these voices are completely real. Sometimes there are a number of voices coming from either inside the head or from just outside it, or from both at the same time. The voices usually bully and intimidate, threaten and harass. Think of the most horrible and upsetting thought or deed you've ever experienced; think of your most abject failure. Then just imagine the effect of voices constantly reminding you, nagging you, warning you, that they will take revenge. The voices will see nothing but negatives in anything you do. The voices will threaten you with dire consequences. The voices will pursue you night and day, giving you no peace, no privacy and absolutely no sense of self-worth. Try to live a normal life in the company of these terrible voices. It's not easy.

Delusions are also classed as positive, "extra", symptoms. There are many types of delusions, the grandiose ones being the most talked about. "He thinks he's Napoleon," is an example given to the uninitiated. In reality, this type of delusion is rarer than others. I have never come across anyone thinking they were a named famous person, alive or dead, although I did come across sufferers thinking they were connected to a famous person, or at least that they were "unknowingly" famous.

Niall suggested I ought to have a chat with Tom, a patient on Ward 2. I had been struggling to understand delusions. "Tom'll put you right. Just ask him about his worries. He loves to tell anyone about them." So it was that one weekend, when Tom wasn't working on the Farm Group, I asked him if we could have a cup of tea together and a chinwag after breakfast. I had spent little time with Tom previously. He was a loner, like so many others, preferring to sit watching TV. Like all the other patients, he'd been resident in the hospital for years. Middle aged, he wore a cloth cap, he'd have had it for years, and a shaggy moustache that he allowed us to trim only occasionally. He wasn't a pacer of the corridors. When he was on the ward, he usually just sat in the day room watching TV.

I had noticed that he appeared to talk to the TV, at times standing up and shouting at people on the screen, usually news presenters or politicians. I am prone to do the same with infuriating presenters, so just took it that he had reached a level of anger and frustration similar, or perhaps even more, than mine. After introducing myself, I blundered straight in.

"I notice you watch the TV lots. What programmes do you specially like?"

"I 'ate 'em all," Tom snapped. He took a long drag of his rolled up cigarette, pulling the smoke in deep, holding it there. The smoke returned in billows as he spoke.

"If you hate them all so much, why watch?"

"I've got to. No fucking option."

"Do the programmes worry you?"

"You've got no fucking clue what's going on, have you? I wish I could be like you. But I know what's going on. It's just that I can't stop it."

"Have you always been like this with TV?" I was struggling to understand his line of thinking.

"Nah. Used to quite like TV, when I was younger. Then I saw it. Not fair that. Bastards!"

"What started you worrying about the TV?"

"It's not the TV, it's some of the people on it." He glanced around to make sure no one was eavesdropping. His voice quietened, speaking confidentially to me. "They tell me things. You might not be able to see it, but I know what's 'appening. I 'ave to fucking live with it."

"What do they tell you?"

"Well...... First started when I saw Robert fucking Dougall. 'e was reading the news, as 'e did. I saw 'im pull down his eye, like this." Tom pulled the lower lid of his left eye downwards, as though scratching it briefly. Smoke from his lighted cigarette irritated his eye and he then scratched it more. "That was the sign. But Robert fucking Dougall knew that I had seen 'im do it. 'e knew I knew. Why did it 'ave to be me?"

"Couldn't he have just been scratching his eye?" I asked, trying to push the obvious alternatives to him.

"You didn't see it, no one else in 'ere did. But others knew what 'e meant. Then, a few days later, I was across at the pub 'aving a pint with Charlie and the Landlady did the same. Christ, she's fuckin' dangerous. She was a part of it – she's part of them. And I never fucking knew! All that time in that pub. 'Er! They do this to let each other know that they're in the same group. It's their secret fucking signal. But now I know what's 'appening, I know. They're after me now. I watch the TV trying to find out what they're after. These bastards, they're trying to control me, putting ideas into me 'ead, especially when I'm asleep. I try to stop it 'appening, but they're much more powerful than me. They'll get me in the end. Bastards!"

As he talked I became aware of an itch on my left eye. If I scratched it, would I become one of the conspirators in his dreadful plot? I willed myself not to touch anywhere on my face, let alone round my eye. My concentration was now much more focused, on my actions, or rather lack of actions, than on what Tom was saying.

As the weeks progressed, I became more aware of the depth of Tom's delusion. His delusion grew and grew as the random actions of people, especially those in the public view, innocently touched or scratched themselves as they spoke. Each action was further proof of the sinister spider's web of this dangerous group who were plotting to….. ? Tom didn't know, but it would be cataclysmic. His fear of the group's evil intentions was probably less than his fear of the knowledge that he was the only person who knew what was being hatched. He felt that he was the only one who wasn't a part of this diabolical gang, yet knew of its existence. The intimidation, the sense of threat that he felt, was overwhelming.

On top of this, Tom also heard voices. Needless to say, the voices didn't just confirm his fears but took them to an even higher pitch, confirming his sense of complete and utter isolation.

The final nail in his coffin was that absolutely nobody in authority took any notice. His dire warnings went completely unheeded.

"All they ever do is stuff me full of fucking medicine, as if that's of any use," he told me one day. "You're all doomed. The lot of you."

Delusions are defined as "fixed, false beliefs". Yet as I came to know patients with delusions their base always seemed to be connected to electricity or electrical devises. Throughout my time as a student nurse we used to wonder what had sparked the delusions before the days of electricity, as so many of the delusions we encountered seemed to involve this medium. For example, we came across many patients who believed that the television, or the radio, or aerials and power lines were somehow implanting terrible thoughts into their heads, against their will. As student nurses we considered that these delusions, which seemed so common in the schizophrenia of the 1970s, had to be connected to what was happening in the world at that time. What had delusions consisted of prior to the harnessing of electrical power? Then I came across the story of James Tilly Matthews.

James Tilly Matthews wasn't the first person with schizophrenia, but he was the first to have a book written about him. His is the first fully documented case of schizophrenia and he is "quite a case". Was he a spy, a double agent, or perhaps just a clever con man? Or was he severely mentally ill?

Matthews was a tea-broker, a very wealthy man in the late 1700s, wealthy enough to break free from his profession and travel to France with the intention of ensuring peace continued between Britain and France. Initially the ruling French parties trusted him, but with the rise of the Jacobin faction he was accused of being a spy and put in jail. Three years later, having narrowly escaped the guillotine, he was repatriated to England as a lunatic, even as the Reign of Terror was underway in France. Returning to Britain he accused the Home Secretary, Lord Liverpool, and the William Pitt administration of treason, not doing himself any favours by making this a public accusation in Parliament. This outburst was enough to get him admitted to Bethlem Hospital. His troubles had only just begun.

His family fought hard for his freedom and release, employing two independent doctors to assess him, both of whom were unequivocal in their belief in his sanity. Release was denied by government decree. Lord Liverpool, perhaps not coincidentally, was the signatory to his continued incarceration.

John Haslam, the effective controller of Bethlem, wrote a book describing Matthews' mental state, as a response to the two independent doctors assessment that Matthews was sane. Haslam was convinced of Matthews' insanity and to prove this his book described Matthews' delusions, his fixed, false beliefs.

The delusions involved an "Air-loom" run by a gang, whose leader was 'Bill' or 'The King'. The "Air-Loom Gang" implanted thoughts in others through "pneumatic chemistry". The driver of this pneumatic chemistry was an elaborate machine, the Air-loom. The Air-loom was drawn by Matthews (and has, in the last decade, been built in Newcastle, although not working!) and described by Haslam. The size of a small room, it was a wooden box with tanks on the sides. Into these tanks noxious fluids and gasses were introduced, including seminal fluid, from men and women, effluvia of copper and dogs, stinking human breath, the plague, gas from the anus of a horse, Egyptian snuff, arsenic, poison of toad and a carnation! This would generate power to force thoughts from the Air-loom out into the atmosphere and then into people's heads, turning them into ..... Matthews was vague about this.

While Haslam was writing a book about Matthews, Matthews was writing a book about Haslam. The result was that Haslam was eventually sacked from his position in Bethlem. Matthews was at last released from Bethlem after 17 years and admitted to a private hospital, where he died in 1815. Looking back it is difficult to get any clear answer on the question of Matthews' sanity. His delusions seemed to have been complex and multi-layered. Why some professionals thought he was quite sane, while others were totally convinced of his insanity makes you wonder. Was the whole thing politically motivated? Matthews' story remains a fascinating description of delusion from yesteryear. His story comes from long before the days of beaming radio waves, and other more sinister rays, through the ether. But delusions so often involve the manipulation of scientific equipment.

Both Tom's and Matthews' delusions have a great deal in common.

Given that schizophrenia usually first appears when sufferers are in their twenties, and rarely shortens life, the torments continue for decades. Although most of us talk to ourselves from time to time, to see someone appearing to have a full-blown conversation with themselves in the street can be quite disturbing. You are possibly seeing someone with untreated schizophrenia. Most severe untreated illnesses lead to decline and eventual death. Schizophrenia, in itself, is never fatal, but the ongoing mental torture will feel more like death in life.

Before the introduction of anti-psychotic drugs, the only way to find peace, for many sufferers, was suicide.

# CHAPTER TEN

For centuries there had been no relief for sufferers of schizophrenia. Many treatments had been tried, but no satisfactory solution had been found. Most treatments fell back on either exhaustion or restraint. Tire them out with activity, strap them into a straightjacket or pin them in either an ice-cold or alternatively, a very hot bath with a lid they couldn't open. If it did nothing else it exhausted them. Nothing seemed to work.

As the twentieth century began so treatment progressed from the cloth straightjacket to the chemical straightjacket of medications, such as the barbiturates or Paraldehyde, medications used to send them to sleep, to tranquillise them, to exhaust them, but not medications to treat their troubled condition. When they woke they were no better; they merely had had some temporary rest from the voices that plagued them and the false beliefs and fears that they lived with.

Insulin, used for sufferers of diabetes, was tried as a treatment for schizophrenia. It was used as a "coma" treatment, a method of inducing deep sleep, followed by a dextrose infusion to wake them. If nothing else, the treatment would allow the sufferer a break from the hallucinations and delusions, albeit in a deep sleep state. This treatment continued well into the 1960s.

By the 1920s, clutching at straws, it was thought that schizophrenia was probably linked to epilepsy, although no one seemed to be able to demonstrate a link. The only link I could ever find was that both groups of sufferers had received similar appalling abuse from the church for centuries. People with epilepsy seemed to improve after having a seizure, but would slowly deteriorate again until the next seizure. Therefore, it was postulated, a convulsion induced by physicians might be a good thing. So why not try giving them seizures artificially? Shock treatments were the proposed solution.

Initially the method used for the induction of a seizure was camphor and cardiazol, first documented medically in 1934. This created a convulsion in the patient after being administered. The problem with this treatment, apart from the risk of a chemically induced shock, was that the treatment took a considerable time to induce a convulsion, half an hour or more. Often the patient had wandered off, so the convulsion was unsupervised and un-noticed, except by the patient.

Insulin Coma Treatment developed into Insulin Shock Treatment, the next of the shock treatments used in the asylums. When insulin was given by injection, it reduced the blood sugar to dangerous levels, leading to seizures as the body shut down. Almost at the point of death, dextrose solutions would be given via a tube through the patients nose to their stomach, to save life. Once consciousness was regained, insulin would be re-administered. Death was a not uncommon result of this flaky treatment. Even those who survived showed no improvement, but the goal was still to induce seizures. A safer method needed to be found.

...........................................

It had been thought for decades that fits could be induced by electricity. Surely, if nothing else, this would save time and money on the costly insulin shock treatment, the only method available to induce fits. A Dr Cerletti had noticed that pigs in an abattoir, prior to having their throats slit, were given a large electric shock to render them unconscious. However, if they avoided the knife, they would usually recover. Dr Cerletti wondered if a severe electric shock, leading to unconsciousness, would "tranquillise" patients with schizophrenia. Neurophysicians only needed a gentle hint to try anything, however bizarre.

In 1937, the Italian Dr Cerletti and a colleague subjected a gentleman who'd been mute for some months, with an unknown condition, to the first Electro Convulsive Therapy (E.C.T.). Years later the colleague would describe that first E.C.T. The doctors didn't know how much electricity to pass between his temples so just wound up the volts until a seizure resulted. The records from this first E.C.T. show that once the patient had had the seizure he was quiet and still for some time. Regaining consciousness he sat up and said, "What the fuck are you arseholes trying to do?" Fair comment!

The major boon for this treatment at the time was that the seizure could be induced instantly, at the touch of a button, so at least the convulsion was monitored and controlled. A box, the Ectonus machine, triggered the voltage surge. Simple.

Despite the lack of any evidence either that schizophrenia was related to epilepsy, or that there was benefit in giving someone with schizophrenia an epileptic seizure, the procedure grew in popularity. If it was used for one condition, why not try it for all? Depression, anxiety, schizophrenia, aggression, mania, obsessions. You name it, it was tried. After about thirty years it was finally accepted by psychiatrists that E.C.T. had no positive effects on schizophrenia. When anti-psychotic medications arrived E.C.T. was eventually abandoned as a treatment for schizophrenia.

What about surgery? Could this be used as a treatment for schizophrenia? People who had had accidents, causing damage to the frontal lobe of the brain, seemed to be less aggressive and more compliant. Why not try surgery for schizophrenia? So metal frame structures were developed to fix the head firmly to enable small holes to be drilled on each side of the head, the temples. Through these holes a thin wire was inserted, then heated to white hot, given a wiggle and, lo and behold, the main structures of brain tissue in the frontal lobe were burned out. The person was, not surprisingly, much quieter after this. The lobotomy had been invented.

But this was an expensive treatment, both in manpower, operating room time and fitting the metal frame. Walter Freeman, an American doctor now generally loathed, worked out the frontal lobotomy method in the mid 1940s. He had been practicing with an icepick (a metal javelin about ten inches long) and experimented with grapefruits and dead bodies, before announcing to the world that the operating theatres were no longer needed, just the icepick – oh, and a hammer! By inserting the icepick round, and then behind, the eye, and then using the hammer to knock through the orbital bone at the back of the eye socket, he could reach the frontal lobe. By then wiggling the ice pick he would sever the main connections of the lobe, before withdrawing. He would then shift to the other eye. Sometimes, almost as a circus act, it was done in both eyes simultaneously. Mostly this procedure was undertaken immediately after a session of E.C.T., when the patient was in a stupor, so there was no need for anaesthesia. Photographs were taken, almost advertising the procedure, showing a man with two ice picks protruding from his eyes. Now there's salesmanship!

The inventor of the lobotomy procedure won a Nobel Prize and, with the quick methods of Walter Freeman, thousands were wheeled into doctors' surgeries for this procedure to take place; simply, easily, dangerously. Children were lobotomised for hyperactivity. People with learning disabilities were lobotomised to make them less noisy. "Bring them all in" seemed to be the motto. President Kennedy's sister was lobotomised at the secret instigation of her dreadful dictatorial father, Joe. She never spoke or functioned properly again, dying some years later. Rose, her mother, was never consulted about the plan for her to undergo this terrible treatment. The problems of the lobotomy became more and more apparent, changes to the personality, brain damage, physical and mental incapacity and, of course, death. By the late 1960s the lobotomy had fallen from favour. Indeed, even the Soviet Union under Stalin banned it as a treatment as early as 1950. There were pressures to rescind the Nobel Prize but these were rejected. The lobotomy treatment is now universally condemned.

Given the total failure of other treatments, psychiatry fell back on prescribing medication. Medication was used either to sedate and tranquillise, or sometimes to punish. Drugs such as the barbiturates and a particularly offensive drug named Paraldehyde were given to "flatten" someone who was out of control. Paraldehyde had two extra negatives for everyone involved. Firstly, it had to be given through a glass syringe, with a metal connector between the syringe and the needle, as the drug would burn through plastic. So, what would it do to sensitive bodies? Therefore it was more complicated to administer, as well as dangerous. Secondly, patients on the drug tended to sweat it out of their systems, and a sickly odour would pervade any ward where it had been administered. These drugs were used as a chemical "cosh". But in the 60s there were other unpleasant ways of control, often considered local "delicacies". The Black Strap at St. Paul's was just one of many local "remedies". Most asylums had their own odd brews.

We look at these barbarous treatments today with horror, yet we have to be careful as we cast our eyes back. These were different times and somewhere in this morass was the ongoing quest for the Holy Grail, a treatment that really worked for schizophrenia.

Schizophrenia was costing more and more. The damage done to the sufferer, and the problems communities had in maintaining someone with schizophrenia in their midst, led to ever greater numbers being placed in the asylums. By the 60s the costs of maintaining the asylums was nearing the cost of the whole of the rest of the NHS.

In addition, there was still no therapeutic treatment for schizophrenia, just methods of control and restraint. Nothing stopped the voices, the delusions and the eternal pain of the sufferer.

It took the French to come up with a treatment, and, like just about everything else in psychiatric treatment, it only happened by chance.

# CHAPTER ELEVEN

Bob and Jack often spoke in horror of the enforced activities in the hospital theatre. As student nurses they, and those in their care, had been forced to attend a matinee every Wednesday afternoon. "Get them all there, no exceptions," were the instructions of the old charge nurses. "Strictly Come Dancing" was an order rather than a pleasure. Student nurses and junior staff had to insist on the attendance of all patients, no excuses, and take them to what was disparagingly called "The Idiots Ball".

Once there, the male patients and male nurses would sit on two sides of the hall. The female patients and female nurses on the other two. The hospital's limited collection of scratched singles would bleat feebly from an old gramophone on the stage. Staff and patients would sit impassively, enduring two hours of boredom until allowed to return to their wards.

At some point during the interminable afternoon, the chief male nurse or his deputy would drop in, see the patients and staff sitting round the edge of the hall and ask why no one was dancing. The closest student nurse, with the enthusiasm of someone being instructed to make a complete fool of themselves, would take one of his patients by the hand and walk round the hall. As they reached the female side a female student nurse and female patient, also hand in hand, would link to the male pair and the walk would continue. As they progressed round the theatre, each side would add two more to the line.... two more males... two more females.... If the chief male nurse stayed long enough an ever lengthening single line would be walking hand in hand, heads down in silent resentment, clockwise around the hall. There was absolutely no connection to the beat of the music and no sense of rhythm; it was a compulsory line-dance for the rhythmically disinclined.

The minute the chief left everyone would rush back to a seat, an unplanned game of musical chairs. All would sit immobile until 4 o'clock. Only then could they escape, back to their wards. At least it would be another week before these futile wanderings recommenced.

............................

Just three weeks after starting on Ward 2 there was a staff dance in the theatre. I can remember no other while I was a student nurse. The theatre had been used extensively in the past, but those days were gone. Although the floor was still polished and buffed and the chairs round the edge were still straightened and dusted, by 1978 the music had faded away.

A band used to playing in smoky pubs, not large echoing theatre halls, had been booked. The staff had high expectations of the band, expectations that were quickly shattered. Staff and their partners had come to chat, dance and show off their posh frocks. Although all of my friends were sitting in their usual places in the bar downstairs in the Social Club, I had paid for a ticket so I trudged grudgingly up the steep steps at the back leading to the hall, clutching my pint. I wondered why I'd bought the damned ticket in the first place. It was a waste of the price of three good pints. Unlike others, my expectations of the band were, at least, realistic. They were bound to be useless. The Social Club could only afford "useless", the last Secretary and Treasurer had seen to that. As I entered the hall I could see no obvious space to sit and no one I could converse with. Indeed, I couldn't see anyone at all that I even knew.

Then I saw David. Four couples sat around a table, David organising everything as usual, all very proper. I thought I'd sit with them for ten minutes or so watching the band, before returning to my usual hangout at the bar. David reluctantly acknowledged me and introduced me to his wife, Molly. I pulled up a spare chair and settled. She was just sitting down, showing off her stunning white dress, which, she told me, had just been redesigned from her wedding dress into a new ball gown. It was a multi-layered frock with frills, lace and pretty netting; I pretended interest. I made the excuse that I just wanted to listen to a song or two before going back down to the bar. I knew I wasn't really welcome in their formal little group.

The round tables were covered with stiff paper cloths; the posh linen had disappeared at the time of the last Secretary. Watching the stage performance, if nothing else to avoid dumb conversation with this group, I placed my pint on the edge of the table, not wanting to get it confused with other drinks already there. Unfortunately there was no table below this section of paper tablecloth, so the pint upended, spectacularly spilling its contents over Molly and her posh new frock. Profuse apologies followed, but David and Molly had to go home. She was completely drenched. I quickly returned to the bar eager to refill my glass and be back among friends. My relationship with David and friends was irretrievably damaged. The incident was never mentioned again. This was always a bad sign.

..............................

It was my first drug round. Unfortunately it was with David. After the disastrous episode of the staff ball I knew there would be scant support from him

After my four years at University I considered that dispensing and understanding medications would be relatively simple. I quickly learned the error of my ways. It was lunchtime. The meals were coming out of the kitchen on trolleys and being distributed by other staff. The medicine trolley was collected from the clinic and the keys passed to me. Inside four tiers of small bottles faced me. The medicine cards were propped on the upturned lid, like a score on a piano, except that this score was even more difficult to read. Each bottle had a different name, which meant nothing at all to me, a name that often even failed to correspond to the name on the medicine card.

With the trolley lid open, a number of the patients stood up to form an orderly queue.

At the front of the queue stood Harry, right behind the lid of the trolley. He was always first in the queue. It was his place. Anyone getting to the front before him would be rudely pushed out of the way. All the patients knew their place in the pecking order.

I am ashamed to say that one of my first "brilliant" ideas was to use a bell to indicate the start of the process, rather than shouting: "Medicine time, come and get it!" Quite rightly I was slapped down.

It was only later that Jack giggled at my idea, "I think you'll find that Pavlov screwed up that idea a hundred years ago."

STUART TOWNSEND

He was correct. Pavlov had experimented with dogs, showing that ringing a bell when feeding was due to start could, in itself, create salivation in the dogs, even when food was not forthcoming. This became known as Operant Conditioning. Bell ringing for patients in the asylum was a really bad idea.

Harry's frustration was beginning to show as he waited for his medication. "Get a move on Master". His was the first medication card. David helped, dispensing the tablets that Harry swallowed without water, relying just on his saliva to help them slip down.

Each medication had two names, a trade name and a generic name. So the trade name might be Serenace, but the generic name would be haloperidol, just as paracetamol is sold as Panadol. Sometimes the bottle would have the trade name and sometimes it would have the generic name. Sometimes, just to further increase the chance of a cock-up at medicine time, the name given on the medicine card was a trade name and the name on the bottle was a different trade name, despite the fact that they were exactly the same drug. My first drug round took so long that some of the patients gave up waiting and wandered off.

When I asked what each drug actually did, or what it was supposed to do, both David and Niall would give loose answers. "It's for sleep," or "it's to keep them calm." Niall would give a couple of answers before losing patience and snapping irritably, "it's 'cause they're fucking mad," which meant that he'd reached the limit of his explanations.

The drug that seemed to crop up most often was chlorpromazine, with a trade name of Largactil. Niall, who had been a nurse for about two decades, told me how widely used this drug had become since he started. "The old charge nurses

88

used to put it into the teapots. They didn't bother with exact doses. Everybody got it. Unless, of course, they didn't drink fucking tea."

Chlorpromazine was the one treatment that changed psychiatry. It changed everything we did. It was our "Road to Damascus". Only later was it found that this panacea had some terrible side effects.

Everyone had continued to look for a simple and effective treatment for schizophrenia. The surgical and shock treatments had failed. The medicinal treatments just sent patients to sleep, a narcoleptic response only! The costs in both distress and taxpayers money continued to rise. Still there were no solutions. People with schizophrenia were still tormented with voices, thought disorders, delusions. Was there ever going to be any answer? The search for an "anti-psychotic drug" continued.

Drug companies always look for a high profit drug. In the period just after the Second World War big profits were being made with the anti-histamine group. These were medications given for allergic responses, such as asthma or hay fever.

A new drug, promethazine, was developed under the trade name of Phenergan. When tested it was found to have only limited effect on allergies. But some of the testing was done within French asylums - where else could you test drugs and not have too many questions to answer if people died? The results were nothing short of amazing. As an anti-allergy drug it was no better than any other, but remarkably many patients with the hallucinations and delusions of schizophrenia, who had been taking this drug to test its safeness for allergic remedy, stopped having these active symptoms. They were free. The breakthrough had occurred.

Chlorpromazine, also called Largactil (or Thorazine in the USA), was developed from promethazine. In high doses it put people to sleep, so it was initially marketed as a "chemical lobotomy", a great selling point! However, it was found that at lower doses it didn't send people to sleep, but reduced and often stopped the hallucinations and delusions, the thought disorders of schizophrenia. Never before or since had one drug so changed psychiatry.

There was a rush to produce chlorpromazine so that by the early 1960s it was being used in almost industrial quantities in the west. Britain's asylums had just been given their terminal status. The combination of the new Mental Health Act, which removed the walls and gave patients rights of their own, and chlorpromazine, which successfully treated schizophrenia, was the death knell for the asylum.

Patients could now go home.

The asylums emptied by two thirds. Chlorpromazine was everywhere, given by tablet, syrup or injection, or just dissolved in the big teapot used in all the wards. The tea was poured into thirty of forty cups and drunk by all the patients. No refusals were accepted. The early days of chlorpromazine would see the charge nurses pacing around at mealtimes, a tin pencil case in hand. Inside sat three sizes of white chlorpromazine tablets, 25, 50 and 100 milligram. The charge nurse would move from table to table choosing what dose to give. "I think you need a big pill today," he would say, carefully taking out a big pill and ensuring it was swallowed, before moving on. In those days there were no medication cards to complete. The prescription would be in the patient notes, usually just the medication name. It was up to the charge nurse to choose how much to give. It often depended how quiet a shift he wanted.

So chlorpromazine allowed patients who suffered the torments of hell to restart a more normal life, to have conversations with fellow humans, rather than the voices in their heads. The revolution had taken place and all seemed positive. The first anti-psychotic drug was now in place.

Yet, like most panaceas, the dark side had yet to appear. For some it actually stopped the delusions and hallucinations. For others it merely reduced them, leading to psychiatrists increasing the dosages, trying to get better results, which in turn led again to tranquillisation and massive irreversible side effects. For about a third of patients it had no anti-psychotic effect at all. As time went on side effects increased: the peculiar walk, the mouth and jaw movements, the restlessness, the problems with vision, the weight gain, as well as the tiredness, apathy and withdrawal. The sedation. These side effects often only showed themselves after a decade or more of taking the new medication. It was found that the new medication damaged the extra pyramidal tract in the brain, an irreversible damage. The effects of the drug, for some, gradually became as disturbing as their untreated original symptoms. Those who suffered most were the one third for whom the anti-psychotic medication had no effect at all. This led to psychiatrists prescribing huge doses, resulting in massive side effects, in addition to the original symptoms, which were still untreated.

By the time I started, in 1978, the negative effects of the anti-psychotics were still being brushed under the carpet. Various new medications were given in conjunction with the anti-psychotics just to counter the side effects. But the new medications, with their new side effects, didn't actually treat the most damaging side effects of the anti-psychotics, as most of the long term side effects of the anti-psychotics, especially the damage to the extra-pyramidal tract, were found to be totally untreatable.

As the asylums emptied another problem arose. Twenty years earlier the asylums had a range of patients with various illnesses. With the new medications and the Mental Health Act the flavour of the asylums had changed. Those remaining were mostly the unlucky few who had no chance of getting out. The long stay wards were now more volatile, with just the most damaged and dangerous remaining.

Many senior managers of the old asylums made a fortune setting up their own private residential homes and then transferring their own well-behaved long stay patients to their own private care. The new institutions, free of government interference, grew in size, but at little cost difference to the taxpayer. Initially the outcome was even more institutionalisation.

The "Idiots Ball" had gone, but for some years many discharged patients would wish to go back, even if it was only for the compulsory line dancing.

# CHAPTER TWELVE

Group Psychotherapy, a phrase glibly used to describe any form of organised interaction without medication, had been around for decades. "One Flew Over The Cuckoo's Nest" was a brilliant example of how this supposedly harmless, non-medical treatment could go disastrously wrong. Encouraging patients to "open up" in a group situation has real dangers. Getting the toothpaste out of the tube is easy. What to do with it, once it is out, is somewhat more problematic. Forcing it back into the tube is impossible. Why does anybody keep toothpaste in a tube? Because, in the tube, it is safer. Even patients in the asylums understood that some things were best kept to themselves. No one wanted to divulge information that might be used against them. Group psychotherapy could be a minefield.

Being a group psychotherapy virgin, I was determined to ensure that group "psychotherapy" led by me would be as low key and non-intrusive as possible. Yet, even then, I was aware of the potential for things to go wrong. Errors in "getting patients to open up" could be just as damaging for a patient as errors in medical or physical intervention.

David, angling for a soft job at the School of Nursing, could see that I might be useful in advancing his prospects. He suggested that I should start a small "discussion group" to develop "patient interaction" and plan some interesting days out. He chose the patients for me; I was to start the group the following week. Niall, and other staff, were less than impressed with the whole idea. What would be the point? Once I'd finished my experience, where would that leave the patients? The only person, it was whispered, who would gain from the project, would be David.

At least the three patients he chose showed some slight signs of interaction. Unlike so many of the others they did not suffer from delusions and hallucinations. They had some basic communication skills. Perhaps, under my leadership, we could keep most of the toothpaste in the tube, where it would be so much safer. I had no great expectations of the project.

Sam, about 55, who would now be described a morbidly obese, had few obvious psychiatric symptoms. He had lived at the hospital since his twenties, working on the farm group, but with little motivation or enthusiasm. Sam, as I understood from the Charge nurse of the Farm Group, never did anything energetic. For as long as anyone could remember his only job was to make the tea. At this he was only "satisfactory".

Sam had been chosen as a member of my group because he was more talkative than the other patients, but this didn't mean he had a lot to say. His main pastime was watching TV. He saw this as his role in life. To carry out his duties he even had his own TV chair, which no one else was allowed to use. He wasn't a drinker, so he could afford tipped cigarettes, a real luxury. Being large, he was not easily threatened or intimidated and would protect his stash of posh fags with violence if necessary. Sam also had the privilege of his own side room, with a radio. But, like almost everyone else in this ward, he had no friends.

Sid was about 50, with an unkempt mop of black hair and a dark complexion that accentuated his badly shaven face. He had a typical posture of crossing his arms and resting his head on one of his hands. This meant that his head was always turned sharply to his left, so I had to stand beside him, and not in front of him, in order to look him in the eyes. He was constantly anxious, fearful and perplexed. He was forever asking, "Am I going to be alright?" There were variations to this such as, "Am I going to die today?" and "Do I look alright today?" He would hover just outside the office and, if there were a silence, would jump in with one of these questions. "I'm sure you'll get through the day," was the usual response from staff, but I soon found that his questions would go round and round in irritating circles.

"Am I alright?"

Initially my response would be, "Yes, you're a fine chap," thinking that his original question was simply a question about his demeanour and popularity. But it wasn't.

"So you think I'm going to live through the day?"

"Yes Sid. You'll be fine. No problems."

As time went on I would turn away at this point, as if to say that this line of questioning was finished. But it never was.

"You think I'll die tomorrow then?"

"No Sid, you're in great health. Really! You're one of the fittest on the ward. Including the staff!" Probably a relatively true statement given the amount of alcohol they consumed.

There was usually a pause at this point.

"I may look fit, but I'm not a well man. That's why I'm here. It's only a matter of time. You'll find me dead in bed one day, I'm telling you!"

In more than three years I never managed to have a conversation with him that didn't start and end with talk of his impending death.

You see the problem: short-term reassurance reinforced his need for mid-term reassurance, which meant he demanded long-term reassurance. In his eyes, if he needed that much reassurance, there must be something very seriously wrong.

I couldn't handle this. Others dealt with Sid a little more abruptly. "Fuck off Sid!"

In my years in the asylum I would regularly see Sid wandering the corridor. The conversation was always the same, a tortuous meander through the same dead end streets of his imminent demise. When he died, some years after I left the asylum, I wondered if his last words were, "I told you so!" Sid, like Sam, also had no friends.

Walter, the third member dragooned into the group, presented initially as a fading bank manager being relatively smart and wearing spectacles and a grey suit. He appeared more "normal" than many others and wouldn't have attracted a second glance if seen outside. Yet he had a diagnosis of low intelligence and epilepsy, as well as thirty years of institutionalisation. He maintained his formality, always dressing smartly. However, this didn't protect him from cleverer and stronger patients. They saw him as a "soft touch". He was the middle-aged Walter from the Beano Comic, the Softie. The odd threat and Walter would hand over his cigarettes. Walter wasn't a fighter. He always avoided the more disturbed on Ward 2. He'd help set the tables for meals and clear away afterwards, being paid a small fee for these duties. If Dennis, our ward orderly, was true to his usual indolent form Walter did his job as well. He took further abuse for this work on the ward from the same patients who stole his cigarettes. In the asylum he was one of life's victims.

Despite this, Walter had a girlfriend, Minnie, who lived in one of the female long stay wards. Walter and Minnie had been a fixture for many years and both occasionally talked of marriage, or perhaps others talked of their marriage. Anything to change the routines. A wedding in the asylum would be a real novelty. They could be seen hand in hand at hospital occasions, some new staff nodding and smiling indulgently at them. Yet Minnie, although well over 60 and no oil painting, was hardly a secure catch for Walter.

Charlie was the ever-present threat. A member of the farm group on Ward 5, Charlie was one of the rogues of the ward. He was one of those, years ago, who'd wandered across to the medical superintendent's House to scrounge a cup of tea from Mrs. Eaton on the day the wall was opened. Charlie had more freedom to wander than many. He made the most of his freedom. He was a regular in the scruffy Public Bar of the Cross Keys across the road, where he would beg beer from timid strangers who happened to be present. Always scrounging: tea, cigarettes, food, beer, he also scrounged sex, preferring instant gratification to long-term relationships. This was where Minnie returned to the scene. He soon learnt that for two cigarettes Minnie would meet his weekly sexual needs, no questions asked, no commitment made. Charlie was the silent sexual predator of Walter's Minnie. Walter was aware of this and tried to keep a tight rein on Minnie, but Minnie knew how to play the field. She knew when the coast was clear for a quick tryst with Charlie.

Charlie was a wily character. He and Minnie didn't need a snug hotel room. A sturdy outside wall would, and did, suffice.

Walter viewed Charlie with seething hatred. Charlie viewed Walter as the bloke who would make sure that Minnie was as attractive as humanly possible, the bloke who would buy her shiny trinkets to brighten her drab appearance. He also saw Walter as a source of cigarettes, with the threat of violence ensuring a small but steady supply. It was a sad fact that the cigarettes Walter provided under duress for Charlie, were used to purchase Minnie's sexual favours. I was never sure whether Walter understood the pulling power of his nicotine addiction.

June once asked Minnie whether she felt that it might be a bit hard on Walter coping with her sexual two-timing with Charlie.

"Yeah, but I don't let Charlie kiss me. Only Walter can kiss me," she said, taking the high moral ground, before adding, rather sheepishly, "well, unless Charlie wants to give me another two cigarettes."

Walter, like Sam and Sid, had no friends ....... Well, apart from Minnie.

This group was to meet once a week in an office on the corridor, with the aim of having a cup of tea, a chat, planning some activities. It was here that we met for our first get together. I collected the pot of tea, teacups and a plate of plain biscuits, on a tray with a doily, bought specially for the occasion. The idea was normalisation. I was never sure how "normal" this high tea was. Doilies were not "normal" in my background. On the instructions of David I took a cassette recorder with me for that first meeting.

At the start of the meeting I had plugged in the recorder, which I placed on the floor next to me. The four of us were in the room, with a table in the centre, on which the tray of tea sat. I poured out the tea for everyone and handed round the biscuits. They were taken quickly, worried that any returned to the ward kitchen would be consumed by others, others who'd not had the "hard work" of this "group psychotherapy".

"This is the first meeting of this group," I said, " and so before we start properly I wanted you to be aware of this recorder on the floor next to me. You can see now that the red light is blinking. You see this," I lifted the recorder and pointed to the red light, holding the cassette recorder so that they could all see it. "This red light shows it's recording our voices. It will record this first session so that we are able to look at how the group has progressed from the first meeting to the last. You have nothing to worry about with this recorder. It can't harm you. It just records what we say so that I can compare how well everyone has done by the time of the last session. Is that OK?"

No response, but they all looked hard at the cassette tape recorder.

"Does anyone have any problems with this?" I pointed again to the recorder.

There was no reply, although they all continued to gaze at the recorder, with its red light blinking. I put the cassette recorder on the floor beside me.

"Although we need to plan what we are going to do over the next few months, we need to decide first on a name for the group. This can be any name but it has to be one by which we are all known. So can I have a few ideas for names of this group?" I started.

Complete silence. Further explanation was needed to trigger an appropriate response. "The name of our group will be important to us. Can anyone think of a name we can call ourselves?"

Still no answer. The three patients were only interested in the tea and biscuits, probably working out how many biscuits they could take themselves. Theoretical quizzes were not why they had attended. Each probably hoped one of the others might chip in.

I struggled on. "What activities or interests do you have because we may be able to use a name from this as our group name." I might as well have asked for the formula for Fermat's Last Theorem. There was a silence worthy of a monastery.

"What activities do you all do?"

No reply. I turned to Sam, praying he would at least say something, anything. "Sam, what interests do you have?"

After a few moments Sam said in a monotone, "I go swimming". He turned away, eyeing the plate, hoping to be allowed more biscuits. He gave the impression that this was his lot in the conversation stakes until more biscuits were consumed.

"Great," I said, in relief that someone had, at last, broken the silence. "Can you think of anything to do with swimming that we could use as a group name?"

No response.

"Sam, when you are swimming, what sorts of swimming strokes do you do? Is there any word that we can use for this?"

Still no reply. Sam leant forward and took his fourth biscuit, cramming it into a mouth already full, so much so that some dropped out as he forced the new one into the corner of his mouth. Am I making hard work of this, I wondered?

"What sorts of swimming strokes are there, Sam, which we may be able to use for the name of the group?"

A pause in his chewing, a gaze at the ceiling. "Breast stroke," he responded. My delight at the first word from one of the group was tempered by my concern that "the Breast Stroke club" did not give quite the right impression. For Niall, perhaps. But not for the group. Undeterred I ploughed on.

"What other strokes are there?" I was clutching at straws now.

"Back stroke."

"Any others?"

"The crawl."

The Breast Stroke Club, the Crawlers and the Back Stroke Club weren't going to convey the right impression, I felt. All suggested clubs set up by dirty old men in long coats on dark nights. But I was not giving up.

"Sam, is there any other swimming stroke?"

Sam thought for a while, swigged his tea, took the last biscuit, filled his tea-cup with milk and sugar, but without the tea, as the tea pot was now empty, before saying: "The Butterfly."

I snatched at the response with both hands. "Brilliant suggestion Sam. Shall we call ourselves "The Butterflies?" It was a "eureka" moment. A couple of unenthusiastic nods and it was agreed. We had a name, even though the group had about as much connectivity with butterflies as Mother Theresa had with lap dancing.

"We'll meet every week and plan things to do that will be fun and extra to what you already have," which wasn't saying a lot. "But when we meet we will always have a nice cup of tea and a good chat. Right, we'll meet next week and plan then where we want to go and where we want to visit. Unless there's anything else we'll call it a day today and meet at the same time next week. Thank you everyone for coming. Today I'll take the tray away and wash up the cups. Next week one of you will do this. Thanks for coming. See you next week, same time, same place."

They started to get up. The meeting was over. I turned in my seat and pressed the off button on the recorder. Leaning further away I unplugged the lead, picked up the recorder and stood up. Walter stared at the tape recorder thoughtfully. Pointing to it he at last spoke.

"Well. That fucking heater was crap, wasn't it."?

The tape recorder was off. What a shame it failed to record the only spontaneous statement of the afternoon.

.......................................

It was decided soon afterwards that a trip out for the Butterflies, into the city, might be entertaining and so, as it was autumn, a trip to the city pantomime would provide that experience. I would be allowed to take another member of staff with me, but I needed to risk assess. Sid was not good in crowds, and Walter had epilepsy. Sam could get aggressive if confronted and he was rather clumsy. However, nothing ventured... I contacted the Playhouse, asking if there might be any problems I should be aware of. The very accommodating man on the phone told me that there was a scene in the panto with strobe lighting. Strobes have a tendency to trigger seizures, but would it be fair to stop Walter going to the panto for fear of an epileptic attack? I spoke to David who, rather than offering his own solutions, turned the problem back on me, asking for my solutions.

I thought, and then offered my solution to the problem. "We'll go, take Walter, and when the strobes start I'll cover his eyes with the programme." Seemed like a good idea at the time.

The taxi dropped us at the front door of the theatre. It was a matinee performance, but as this was the big city, the fur coats were there in abundance, especially in the dress circle where we'd booked our seats. The kids were in the cheap seats of the stalls or the upper circle. We were in the posh area. Kids and my group would be too much of a potential flash point.

Crowds were not Sid's strong suit. Stairs and heights made things even worse. Given Sid's fear of imminent death this was an area I hadn't bargained for. Sam went first, up the sweeping gold trimmed staircase, irresistibly drawn to the ice creams which he knew were waiting at the summit. I followed. Sid followed nervously, then Walter and Gill, the nursing assistant. Coming down were the crowds who'd already bought and were busily eating their ice creams; Sam was already drooling.

Halfway up the stairs the hustle and bustle of the crowds became all too much for Sid, who stopped, turned and froze when he saw the jostling throng way below him in the foyer. He didn't do heights. Clinging to the banister for support he was petrified.

Sam had joined the queue for ice creams. I became aware that no one was following me. Walter, never good with his sight, bumped into Sid, who was now a statue. Sid was going nowhere. He clung to the banister as though his life depended on it. Those descending were pushing past us, quite unaware of a developing flash point. I had a sudden sense of impending disaster. Walter was at his wits end. He could not get past Sid, so he pushed him. Sid turned and lashed out at Walter, but Gill caught his flailing arm before it could make contact. Walter squared up to Sid, ready for the fray. Meek though he looked, Walter always felt he was a match for Sid. He knew Sid was not keen on being wounded. It would be yet another injury to Sid's ever deteriorating physique. I got between them before further blows could be landed.

"Get a fucking move on. Get out of the way!" Walter screamed.

"I can't move. Who are all these people? Why are they here? I'm not well, you know," wailed Sid, for all to hear. The milling crowds were suddenly aware of this unseemly fracas half way up the stairs. As if by magic space cleared around us. Their ice creams were turning sour. There was a bitter taste in their mouths. Things were turning nasty. The well to do realised they needed to give us space. Their afternoon spree was approaching ruin.

"Sid, Sid, Sid! It's OK, honest, it's OK, just follow me," I urged. I prised his hands from the banister, holding them very firmly. Reassuring him that he wasn't about to die, I was able to lead him up the remaining five stairs. All eyes were still on us. The immediate threat was over.

Clutching a programme and an ice cream, Sam was on his second, we sat in the middle of the Dress Circle watching the panto. It was well underway and everyone seemed to be mesmerised. This calm was only maintained until the strobes started. It was the type of flickering that makes you think of a 20s movie, but it made me think of Walter, sitting on my right, throwing a grand mal seizure. I grabbed my programme and put it in front of Walter's eyes. He brushed my hand down and I tried to push his hand away. I repositioned the programme, right in front of his eyes. The music, at that stage, stopped, the action was in silent movie mode, with just the flickering lights. Walter took the silence as his cue to complain.

"What the hell do you think you are doing? I'm trying to watch. Have you gone completely fucking mad?" Walter didn't usually shout, nor was he usually coarse, but he made an exception this time. The statement echoed round the theatre. Everyone in the dress circle turned to see a young man apparently trying to restrain a meek old gentleman sitting next to him, who was being stopped from viewing the wonderful spectacle. I was now a thug wrecking their outing, as well as harassing an older man. It would be a lot less conspicuous if he had a grand mal seizure. It would certainly be quieter. I put the programme down and let him watch. He loved it.

My greatest fear during any trip to the Panto was that one of the Ugly Sisters would drag a patient onto the stage during the performance. It never happened of course, but with their, and my, lack of control it always felt as if it was a disaster waiting in the wings.

Cinderella was a huge hit for the Butterflies, but it left me with deep psychological scars!

# CHAPTER THIRTEEN

Lack of money is a perennial problem for students. I was no exception. Devoid of savings and with a number of hire purchase agreements to honour, there was never any money left in the pot at the end of a month. The Social Club, not surprisingly, was the major drain on my income. I needed to keep up with the rounds, not wanting to appear a cheapskate, but the charge nurses all drank two drinks to my one. Being taught to play three-card brag made things even worse, especially as my teachers in this sophisticated card game were the very people fleecing me. I never came out in profit. Working Bank Holidays made the difference between total insolvency and just about surviving.

Student nurses in the 70s were paid employees of the hospital, but on a much lower rate than qualified staff nurses. Working Saturdays, Sundays and Bank Holidays could pay up to double the money. So the chance of working over Christmas was an opportunity not to be missed. A late shift Christmas Eve, long day Christmas Day and early Boxing Day would hugely increase my take home pay. God, I needed it. Working these two days would also give me the chance to travel home on Boxing Day to be with family in Derbyshire.

Ward 2 was festooned with the tatty old decorations that no else wanted to use. But everything was as ready as it could be. On Christmas Eve I did a late shift with June. Christmas Day I was to do a long day with June and Niall, from 7am to 8pm. With those two in charge I had no expectations that it was going to be a 'dry' shift.

Christmas Eve had ended with a heavy session down the club, so it was that at 7am on Christmas morning I made my unsteady way down the corridor to the office of Ward 2. I passed Uppa's room. He was getting up, but apart from him there was no sign of anyone. The office was empty. The day room was empty. I checked my watch – five past seven. Where was everyone? I went back to Uppa, got him up, washing and dressing him. Still no one about. The Marie Celeste sprang to mind. A few patients started to appear, but no still sign of Niall, June or Dennis, our orderly. The night staff had gone, the night report was done, but had the day staff been beamed up? I went to the stairs leading to the upstairs dormitory and rooms. The cleaner's room was on the left. I could hear laughter.

Opening the door, I found Niall, June and Dennis there, looking as if they had been not just sampling the alcohol but trying to down the lot. The supply in the room was truly awesome – beers, lagers, wines, whiskeys, gin, vodka, rum – the lot! I helped myself to a beer, despite being encouraged to get into the gin.

Slowly, very slowly, the day progressed. Following breakfast, and some carols and present opening, the patients receiving cigarettes and underwear, the staple Christmas gifts they were used to, the staff again settled back to the alcohol. It looked as if the day would be quiet, hopefully with time for a little sleep in the afternoon.

At midday I reached for another beer. I was still many units behind the others. As I pulled the ring to open the can Niall received a phone call from Ward 14. They had a gentleman on the ward who'd gone into retention. He was unable to empty his bladder. They needed help. Niall, bless his little cotton socks, volunteered me. Who else? Niall saw it as a little Christmas gift for me to help in this acute situation. He knew my keenness for new experiences, but also knew I was the only one who could be ordered to go. Already tired, this as an experience I could do without. I'd have much rather stayed on the ward for a quiet day. Now it would be a long day, a very long day, but at least it would pay well.

Since my first experience on Ward 14, the sick ward, I had had a good feeling about it. Michael was the charge nurse when I arrived. Michael was rare in that he had a dual qualification, S.R.N. and R.M.N., and was working with the on-duty doctor in the main ward. After greeting me and thanking me for coming, there were discussions about what catheter size should be used, what gel, and whether they needed an 'introducer'. This was all double-dutch to me. All I could do was stand by until instructed to do something.

The patient, Frank, I discovered, had been fitted with a catheter for some months. However, it had become blocked at some point, both in 'time' and in his urethra. The catheter was removed in preparation for a new one to be fitted. Without the catheter his bladder couldn't empty, so was now expanding like a balloon. The problem was in fitting a new catheter. Not an easy task. Michael was wearing latex gloves. An array of tubes, clamps, scissors, bowls, sterile water, swabs and chaos surrounded the bed. A sterile cloth surrounded poor Frank's flaccid penis. Taking Frank's penis tightly in one hand and stretching it to its limit, Michael slowly inserted the new greased catheter into the tiny opening at its tip. After a few moments the tube stopped. Michael pushed harder. Blood started to come up the catheter, first in tiny specks, then in drops, then as a steady flow, forming pools of blood on the "sterile cloth" around the base of Frank's penis. I was beginning to feel queasy and uncomfortable. I put my queasiness down to alcohol.

The doctor, eager to make the most of his rapidly disappearing Christmas Day, looked on in frustration. "This is a waste of time. He's punctured somewhere down there. We need an introducer. He'll have to go to A and E. No point in messing him about any further."

Michael told me to have a glass of wine while he phoned the hospital. I sat in the day room with other staff wondering why they couldn't accompany Frank to A and E instead. They all had glasses of wine, but I'd already had quite a few beers, so I politely refused offers of more. The shift had a lot of hours to run.

Half an hour later Michael reappeared. Frank needed to go immediately to the A and E Unit of the general hospital, as he needed "an introducer for his catheterisation", what ever that meant. As the ward was already understaffed I was to go with him. Frank had been an aggressive character who needed to be accompanied by a male staff member to "protect the public".

"Just stay with him and bring him back when they've finished. Take this letter with you. The ambulance has just arrived," were the only instructions I was given. With that Michael was gone and I was left to cope. By now it was well past lunchtime and I'd not even had breakfast, let alone lunch. I was tired, hungry and fed up.

The ambulance staff had Frank loaded. I went in the back with him, with my stained white coat and a letter regarding the clinical issues. As Frank was heavily sedated, I peered under the blanket to check that his now heavily bandaged penis was not soaked in fresh blood. Once at A and E Frank and I were offloaded and left in the main reception. He still seemed sedated, thankfully showed no signs of waking, let alone of aggression.

At Reception I checked in and was given a number. It would be a long wait. I sat with Frank laid out on a trolley beside me. "What a way to spend Christmas", I thought mournfully. I needed sleep, but with sole charge of Frank I knew full well that if my patient went missing and I was found both comatose and a little drunk, there would be some explaining to do. My career as a psychiatric nurse would be very short. Despite the boredom of the wait, the afternoon was rapidly disappearing. Someone in a suit came to switch on the lights of their impressive Christmas tree, which made ours, on Ward 2, look very shabby in contrast.

I came to a decision. Sidling up to reception I informed the clerk that Frank, although asleep, was known for his extreme aggression. His sedation would be wearing off very soon. Within five minutes we were in a side clinic. We had been moved rapidly up the running order. Bob had taught me this clever ruse. I owed him a drink. Practical advice like this was far more useful than weeks of lectures in the School of Nursing.

I stood with Frank in the clinic looking at the racks of tubes, pipes, needles, and syringes. It all looked fascinating yet completely bewildering. I ran my hands down all the packaging, so many different types, so many different shapes. What were they all for? Were nurses really expected to understand all these bits of equipment, I wondered. Two female nurses entered with a tray, handing me a plastic cup filled to the brim with white wine. "Here. Happy Christmas." I, of course, accepted. One doesn't want to appear churlish on Christmas Day. However, no sooner had the wine appeared than one of them handed me a paper mask telling me to put it on. I could still drink the wine, though it involved having to lift the mask each time I wanted to take a swig. I was uncertain how a "sterile field" could be maintained.

A third nurse then came in pushing a trolley laden with various parcels. It began to feel more and more like Christmas! "What size gloves do you want?" she asked.

"Medium," I told her, not knowing what she was on about.

"Would 7s do?"

"Sure," I responded. Was 7 big, small or what? I had no idea.

"Do you want the introducing catheters now? What size Foley catheter are you wanting to insert?"

The blood drained from my face. I had this sudden sense of fear. Although I was three parts gone, tired, hungry and out of my depth, this nurse thought that I was the doctor! There was no way I could participate in this procedure. But then, with a few drinks inside me ...... it would be interesting....... maybe ......

Before I could land myself in really deep water, a man appeared wearing a white coat. Professionalism had arrived. The nurse now looked somewhat doubtfully at me.

"Who are you?"

"I'm just a psych' student nurse who's accompanying Frank. I'm only here to make sure he gets back alright." The nurses in the room looked relieved. The last thing they needed was a novice doctor to work with on Christmas Day.

The procedure went ahead with me slurping wine in the background, and topping myself up from a bottle I found on the window ledge. It all looked so easy when they did it. Frank slept for most of the procedure. The blood ceased its copious flow, which was a relief. With his new catheter fitted, he and I were returned to the waiting room, to wait for an ambulance to return us to the asylum. But it was Christmas Day and ambulances were in short supply. So it was not until 10 o'clock that we finally got back to St. Paul's Hospital. I was tired, hungry and thoroughly fed up.

However, I wasn't too tired to go to the Social Club for a couple before getting home to bed. But even the Club was empty. Everyone had gone home for the end of Christmas Day. I had to be up for a 7am start, but at least I could claim 15 hours of double time. It had been an eventful day, the most peculiar Christmas I'd ever had.

Back in my room I munched on a few Ritz crackers, my only poor stand-in for a Christmas Day turkey.

Reflecting on my day I felt I'd had a pretty poor Christmas, despite the money. But rather my Christmas Day than Frank's.

# CHAPTER FOURTEEN

Giving an injection would be easy, or so I thought. Just a little prick. It proved to be another painful lesson, not just for me but also for the patient.

When chlorpromazine arrived, in the late 50s and early 60s, it was administered almost across the board. For the first time a true "anti-psychotic" drug had been developed. This was not just a drug to send someone to sleep but a drug that actively combated the delusions and hallucinations. It was a remarkable revolution. Many patients who had been thought of as incurable were now living lives free from the terrible thought disorders of untreated schizophrenia.

But these same patients would often have no understanding that they had been ill, feeling instead that their delusions and hallucinations were reality. So, in hospital, they had received chlorpromazine by whatever means, even if it WAS in the tea. For about two-thirds of people with schizophrenia this treatment had worked. They were awake and mostly free from their tormenting demons. There was no longer any need for them to stay in hospital. The exodus had begun. Thousands left to start new lives with a box of chlorpromazine tucked into their "going home" bags to keep them sane.

Once back in the community many ex-patients just stopped taking their medication, often because they saw no connection between their delusions and hallucinations, the asylum and their medication. They had no insight, no understanding of their illness. For most the little white tablets had no purpose. As the exodus accelerated so re-admissions accelerated as well. Without their little white tablets they returned to the asylum, floridly psychotic again, where the frustrated clinicians had to restart their treatment. It proved almost impossible to avoid the "revolving door syndrome".

The solution came from the drug companies, who realised that these types of anti-psychotic medications needed be given in a long acting form by injection. A number of companies developed long acting anti-psychotic medications, made from the anti-psychotic drug and sesame oil. This would be injected into a large muscle for slow release over a period of two to four weeks. These came to be known as "depot injections".

Depot injections were administered by CPNs (Community Psychiatric Nurses), a new role whose sole task was to go out from the asylum and visit the newly discharged patients. Most counties had just one or two CPNs who travelled around with their needles and ampoules, jabbing as they went. I would discover later that our CPN only did his injections in the morning so as not to interfere with his lunchtime drinking sessions, recognising that he would be far too shaky to go 'jabbing in the afternoon'.

Of course, these depot injections were also on the increase in the asylums. In theory they were easier to administer. Also they could be given once a fortnight, instead of having to administer pills four times a day, to patients who were less than keen to take their medication anyway. It was conflict reduction in practice!

About half the patients on Ward 2 had been switched to depot injections, so I needed to learn to give these safely.

A depot injection was quite complicated, needing to be deep and over in seconds. But if it were too deep the needle would hit the bone, sending reverberations up your arm. It was also painful for the poor patient, as hitting the bone would cause the needle to barb, leading to muscle damage on withdrawal. As time went by, giving intra-muscular injections became one of my few strengths. But, when I started, giving injections was a nerve-jangling procedure for me, for the trained nurse and especially for the patient.

We had been briefly taught in the school how to give an injection. We had then each been given an orange and told to practice on it; it was similar in texture to a patient's skin, or so we were told. I found that very hard to believe.

But it was on the wards that I really learned the difference between a human buttock and a Seville orange. First get a syringe (which was in a sealed bag) and two green needles (also in sealed bags). Have these ready with a "sharps bin" (for disposal of the used syringes) and a swab (in a foil sealed container).

In school they had taught us to have the patient lying down on a couch, although in Ward 2 and just about everywhere else, patients stood. To administer the injection an ampoule full of anti-psychotic drug (usually a drug called Depixol or Modecate, similar to chlorpromazine) was drawn up into the syringe. In practice this was easier said than done. Just to get at the drug involved filing away at one side of the ampoule to create a weakness so that the top could be snapped off. But the glass would often shatter, or break in the wrong place, causing me to cut myself and need first aid, so that I'd be back to square one and I hadn't even started! The drug was diluted in sesame oil, which had a similar viscosity to household oil; the small bore of the green needle struggled to drag the drug into the syringe. The plunger of the syringe had to be drawn fully back to fill the vacuum created in the syringe. Once full, the needle had to be changed for a new one as the original one was usually barbed from the pressure of being forced against the base of the glass ampoule. Finally the plunger would be pushed to eliminate any air in the syringe and the injection would be ready.

In reality, given how long this first step had taken, the patient had wandered off, unsure as to why he had to have his trousers around his ankles for such a long time, while I fumbled behind the trolley opening bags and cursing.

Poor Sid from the Butterflies was chosen by David to be my guinea pig, my first stab at a depot injection. Sid was probably picked because he quite enjoyed all the fuss of having an injection. Everything was ready in the clinic when he arrived. A swab was waiting on the trolley, perhaps anticipating problems, such as blood spurting randomly from a badly given injection.

The first problem was the site of the injection. "Give it in the upper, outer quadrant of the buttock." The instructions came with a small line drawing of the rear view of a naked person, hands splayed peculiarly outwards. Across one buttock two lines forming a black cross, with a dot in the "upper outer quadrant". That all seemed quite straightforward until, that is, I had a buttock confronting me. Real buttocks don't come conveniently marked with crossed lines and a target. Without such aids to help me I was lost. Where did the upper half start? Where was the dividing line? Where was the vertical line? Was it halfway between the crack of the bum to the edge of the leg? But where was the edge of the leg? It all depended on where the leg was viewed. The line drawing was too small to discern the exact placing of the cross hairs anyway. The central problem was that bottoms were not two, but three-dimensional. They still are. I wonder how modern nurses cope with this?

This "upper-outer quadrant" instruction was stressed so that nurses would understand the dangers of paralysis if they injected into the sciatic nerve. Quite what the sciatic nerve did, or didn't do, never mind where it was, was beyond me! The warnings were enough to create fear in me. David tapped the spot where he wanted the needle to enter the skin. I focused hard on this spot.

I had been told to use the needle like a dart, pushing it, in one movement, into the fleshy part of the outer buttock. I glanced at the needle, adjusting my grip to hold the syringe like a dart, but I had already forgotten where David had pointed. That first attempt resulted in the needle merely bouncing off his Sid's skin. What a little prick. Sid had had injections for years. His skin was hard and scarred, not at all like an orange. I was sweating heavily. Sid stood still waiting for another prick. I hit the skin again, harder. This time the needle penetrated about a centimetre, but as I tried to force it further in I caused further pain, scything slowly through the muscles of Sid's battered buttock.

"Get a fucking move on," Sid yelled.

I was nowhere near deep enough, so I pulled out. David sighed.

"You've hardly scratched his skin!" he moaned in frustration. "Now you've pulled the needle out it isn't sterile any more. You'll have to start again. You can't go on just tickling him. Get a grip!"

So I started again.

I gathered another needle, took off the wrapping, attached it to the syringe, unsheathed it of its plastic cover and pushed the drug up through the bore to remove any air. David checked the amount of drug in the syringe, but found that instead of 1ml there was now only 0.8ml. I had lost 0.2ml in changing the needle. "Start again" he muttered. "You know these ampoules cost around £25. No more cock-ups please! At £25 a jab we can't afford another mistake."

So I went through the whole drawing up procedure again. Sid, by now completely bored, had pulled up his trousers and gone for another walk down the corridor. David retrieved him. This time I plunged the needle in, but again it stopped after about a centimetre – still not deep enough. David pushed me away angrily, took hold of the syringe, now dangling precariously from the top of Sid's buttocks, and quickly thrust it in to its full depth.

David motioned me to take over again so I grasped the syringe. As the needle was in Sid's buttock to its correct depth all I now had to do was withdraw the plunger slightly, to check that it wasn't in a blood vessel – it wasn't – and then slowly press the plunger home. I held the body of the syringe, and pressed the plunger. The small bore of the needle, combined with the thick fluid of the injection, and the lack of space in the swollen muscle, made it almost impossible to press home the plunger. I pushed harder and harder. The plunger moved painfully slowly, especially for Sid. My hands were sweating. I was having trouble gripping the shiny plastic. I pressed even harder, wondering whether this could be the longest injection in medical history. By this stage I felt I was exerting enough pressure to split the atom.

It was all too much for the equipment. A spray of oil hit me in the face as needle and syringe separated, exploding the viscous fluid around the clinic. I had failed to ensure that needle and syringe were locked tightly together.

David sighed, took control and did the injection again, properly and professionally. It was a real downer. Surely I could get the hang of this? It couldn't be that difficult.

It was only thanks to the patience and perseverance of many different staff that I finally got to grips with it. Once I felt confidence in the process I was asking to inject anyone, anywhere, at any time.

But for the moment Sid was none to pleased about his sore bottom. He later told June that he would rather she did it next time. He also kept asking me whether I thought he would survive, showing me the bruising whenever he had the opportunity. "See, it's still not healed. Probably won't ever heal. It'll become septic. I'll die 'cause of you."

What reassurance!

Giving an injection was an art form that took me many attempts to perfect. I can still feel the pain of many of the patients who suffered as a result of my clumsiness. But, as time went on, it was an art form that I grew to enjoy. There was a rare sense of satisfaction when patients quietly said to others, "I prefer Stuart to do it. No messing around with him." They should have seen me at the start.

It was a satisfying procedure, but only when it went right!

# CHAPTER FIFTEEN

Life in the asylums had changed more between 1960 and 1978, when I joined, than in any other period of their history. Most of the charge nurses who trained me had started their careers in the bad old days before the 1959 Mental Health Act. Although they seemed old-fashioned to me, these were the people who had been at the forefront of establishing patients' rights, of administering the first anti-psychotic drugs, of dragging the asylums into the modern world.

Bob had a no-nonsense reputation. He was intolerant of patients behaving in a way that deliberately caused trouble or pain to others. When he was a charge nurse on Ward 24, the Acute Unit, Bob had thwarted a patient with a sociopathic personality disorder. The patient had taken his revenge by wandering up to the main road and lying down in the middle, across the white line. Bob had received a phone call to report that a patient was lying in the road and that all traffic was backed up to the main hospital in one direction, and the Nurses Home in the other.

Bob had walked up the drive and seen the tailback of traffic. This was the sort of thing that really got under Bob's skin. Someone, he didn't know who, had called an ambulance, which was parked diagonally across the road. Someone had placed a rug under the head of the apparently collapsed figure. He was just laying there, eyes closed. A couple of people, who Bob didn't recognise, knelt beside the figure talking to him and consoling him. At a short distance some wondered if the figure was dead. Some nearby drivers stood beside their cars discussing whether the man had been the victim of a hit and run accident. Others discussed the situation in terms of time lost, looking at their watches in frustration. Further back car horns blared as angry drivers gave vent to their feelings. The patient had become a talking point.

Bob didn't hang about. There was no psychiatric diagnosis with this patient. He had caused significant harm to others with violent and manipulative behaviour. He was now lying in the road to gain sympathy. He was getting it in spades. Manipulative behaviour such as this was like a red rag to a bull for Bob.

Bob walked up to the patient. He looked at him. In sympathy? He kicked him in the thigh. His only words "Get up!"

The patient opened his eyes, saw the look on Bob's face, stood up, handed the rug to the ambulance man and returned sheepishly to the ward. The onlookers gawped. They had been completely taken in. The patient's bluff had been called. There was no messing with Bob. The Good Samaritans quickly realising their kind-heartedness had been misplaced, returned to their everyday business without a word said. The traffic started to move again.

........................

As time went on during my long stay experience, and with my new found friends in the tennis group, I started to get a feel for the changes that had happened over the previous 20 years. Bob and Jack and many others were "old school", but nothing was what it seemed.

When they had started the hospital was still walled. The asylum was still, very much, "the asylum", a secure institution hidden from the community where staff had free rein to do as they pleased. Yet these new staff members, now charge nurses, had also been there when the walls had come down. They were also present when chlorpromazine first started to be used to treat schizophrenia. If pushed they would talk about their earlier experiences back in the late 1950s, before all the changes. It became apparent that, far from being reactive and resistant to change, they had been the ones who had gone through the real revolution. But these changes were not just about chlorpromazine and walls. They were about attitudes. These staff had seen the overt abuse in the system, but hadn't sustained the abuse as they had moved up the ladder. I soon came to realise that their commitment to change had been the foundation stone for modern psychiatric nursing.

Propping up the bar in the Social Club one evening, I bored Bob with my shaving experience on the sick ward. He listened, which he was particularly good at, especially with a few pints and a chaser inside him. Then he shared with me his first shaving experience in the asylum on an old male long stay ward. It had been his first day on the ward. All the male patients were lined up along the corridor, dressed only in white underpants and vests with SP marked on the back; all clothes were communal then. The charge nurse had given Bob a bowl of shaving soap. Bob had gone from patient to patient, down the corridor, lathering their faces. The charge nurse had then handed him a cutthroat razor.

"You shave the chin and under the lip only, boy. We'll do the rest," was the instruction. "Follow me."

With that the charge nurse had started down the line of wearily compliant patients, shaving the left and right side of each patient's face – one sweep for each side of each patient. Bob had followed doing the chin and under the bottom lip. The staff nurse had brought up the rear, swiping the upper lip. As Bob got to the end of the line he had turned to inspect the results. He'd been horrified to see that all the patients had blood dripping steadily from their chins onto their white vests. Looking closely at the cutthroat razor in his hand, he was horrified to see it had a jagged nick in it.

"You should be more careful, boy. You'll need to improve," was the only reaction of the charge nurse.

As I swigged my pint I felt reassured that my first experience of shaving, albeit of a corpse, had been relatively successful.

...................

Jack's first experience with a razor had been a little different. His father had worked as a nurse in the asylum, so Jack knew some of the staff when he started. His first ward, long stay, everyone's first ward seemed to be long stay, was run by a particularly old style charge nurse who knew Jack's father well. When Jack arrived, just before 7am on his first day, the charge nurse greeted him holding a cutthroat razor in its little sleeve.

"Come with me boy." Jack followed into the ward office. "These floors were waxed about ten years ago. The wax has built up in the corners and the edges. Use this to scrape away the excess and work your way round the office. Come and find me when you're finished." The charge nurse left. Jack was left wondering if he should have complained. He'd come as a student nurse, not a cleaner. But the old charge nurse had a fearsome reputation so he decided against complaining and got down on his hands and knees. An hour later he had scraped round half the office. The charge nurse reappeared and told Jack to get himself through to the kitchen where staff were having a cup of coffee. He was never asked to do the job again. It had been a trial of his unflinching willingness to do as he was told. He had passed the test.

Jack told me, over yet another pint, of his first admission on a geriatric ward. A male patient had been admitted, so Jack had been told to make a written record of his possessions, which he duly did. Once the clothing and other possessions had been logged Jack returned to the charge nurse to check that he had done everything correctly. The charge nurse had the patient's money on the desk in front of him. He counted it out, split it into thirds, gave Jack one third, and pocketed the rest. Jack was at a loss. What should he do? It was a "no win" situation. If he shopped the charge nurse he would never work in the hospital again. He would be unable to prove what had happened. It was just his word against the charge nurse. But if he accepted the money he would be a thief. What should he do? He took the money, but with a heavy heart. This was not what he'd signed on for.

This was far from an isolated case in the early 60s. Extra money could be made in two main ways. The first was in direct cash "won" from patients. Every patient was allocated a weekly allowance. This was either a basic amount if they didn't work in the various schemes, or an enhanced amount to demonstrate their worth in the work details such as sewing, pig farming, gardening and arable farming. This was paid weekly. Once a week the charge nurse would collect all the allowances for all patients from the administration office and, in theory, distribute this money, on a daily basis, to the individual patients. This was the theory. The reality was, as both Jack and Bob remembered it, that the charge nurse would take about 60% of the money. No one would ever be able to prove that this percentage "take" had come from theft. Patients had signed for receipt of the money, but the money had already been "heavily taxed".

However this was just one part of the scam. The second method involved creaming off what they could of the 40% remaining.

Cigarettes were allocated to all patients but were bought from the hospital shop, by the charge nurses, using some of the remaining money. A patient might be allowed money for 20 cigarettes a day, but this allowance would also be severely "taxed". He might receive far less than half his daily due, the remainder being siphoned off for the charge nurse to trade elsewhere. Hence the endless wanderings by the patients in search of fag ends. Jack told me of one occasion when he was helping his patients in the farm group. He had gone to the charge nurse to ask for cigarettes for the morning's work and reluctantly been given one cigarette per patient. He had received the same allocation for the afternoon and the same for the evening. The excess cigarettes became another commodity to be sold outside the asylum. A nice little earner.

Another simple scam was to buy new clothes "for the patients". These clothes were always in exactly the right sizes to fit staff on the ward. Once paid for, out of the patients' allowance, the new clothes would be swapped for old clothes brought in by the staff. "What size shirt do you wear?" was asked of younger staff members. When the new shirts arrived the staff members would simply strip off their own shirts, put on the new ones, leaving the old shirts to become part of the ward stock. The annual audit always showed the correct number of shirts.

The same type of systemised fiddle even occurred with the crockery. Broken crockery could be replaced through the asylum stores. So broken cups, plates and saucers were taken to the stores department and replaced with new in equal number. Charge nurses were tipped off when the broken crockery was due to be taken to the local tip, so junior staff would be sent to the tip to reclaim it, collecting the broken bits just deposited. These would then be brought back to the asylum, distributed to other wards, returned to the stores, and recycled again. This endless recycling system provided many staff with a never-ending supply of brand new crockery, much of which, in turn, provided the crockery for their caravans!

By the time I started, in the late 1970s, these corrupt systems, as far as I could see, had stopped. I heard that Jack had been one of the triggers for the ending of the money scam, having shopped his opposite number for still playing it. Jack had found a large collection of cash in the one lockable drawer of the new ward Jack had taken over. His opposite number was the culprit. The authorities had been informed; the charge nurse had left. The asylum, with the help of those who I thought of as "old school", had started to clean up its act.

Niall told me that a London asylum appointment as a charge nurse could mean as much as £50 a week in profitable take in the 1960s. Many staff had been not just morally reluctant, but financially reluctant, to make way for change. The changes came. With all the charge nurses I worked with there was never any sense that they would rip off the patients. The hospital? Perhaps, often. The Sports and Social Club? YES! The patients? Never.

The old charge nurses who taught me were the steady hands, even with a few drinks inside them. When there was trouble they were there. They were the people you rang to get help. Somehow, with all their years of experience, they seemed hard-wired to understand when a patient needed understanding and gentleness or when a tough and uncompromising approach was needed. I once saw Bob completely diffuse a very aggressive situation just by quietly suggesting that a violently disturbed patient sat down with him, just to talk things through. I cannot remember any situation where he had to resort to pinning someone down, forcibly injecting them. To me these old charge nurses, the "old school", seemed to have a unique blend of authority, awareness, instinct and tolerance.

They were the bedrock of the movement that dragged the asylums out of the dark ages and into the modern world. As a young student nurse they didn't just teach me about the hospital and the patients, they taught me about life.

# CHAPTER SIXTEEN

Geriatric handovers always emphasised the timing of the toileting regime. This must never be broken. One Sunday afternoon, as I was preparing to go off duty, three Filipino staff came to cover the late shift. None of them were regular staff on Ward 7, but they had covered the occasional shifts.

The following day Jack, tennis opponent and my new boss as charge nurse on Ward 7, my new geriatric experience, was summoned to the administration office. On his return he joined us, while we were having a coffee in the Day Room, to explain the issue. The nursing officer, his line manager, had received a complaint. Three relatives of one of the patients, two women and a man, had come to visit the previous afternoon. Whilst sitting with their relative all three had been toileted by the Filipino staff - "You come with us. No make naughty! You do wee-wee!" To make matters worse the visiting ladies had been "hooked" onto the commode and not released until they had visibly performed. The Filipino staff hadn't enough English to understand their cries of complaint.

Interestingly, although the relatives had made a formal complaint, they had been adamant that their only real concern was that there had been just three staff on the ward, none of whom were fluent in the English language. They seemed to accept the compulsory toileting as just another odd part, of another odd visit, to another odd relative! The episode was relived some days later when the gentleman visitor returned for a chat with Jack, asking for "forgiveness" for his complaint. He was apologetic for making any negative comments about the ward, seeing the incident as a highly amusing mistake. I always thought that the Filipino Nurses, that afternoon, must have thought that the toilet round had dragged on longer than usual. They must also have wondered where those "patients" had disappeared to at teatime. As always the asylum did "odd" rather well. Geriatrics was no exception.

This complaint highlighted the rigidity of the routines in a geriatric ward, a rigidity that allowed no dissent. Routines took precedent over logic and reason. Yet routines were the foundations of certain principles: the principle of care, the principle of cleanliness, the principle of adequate diet and hydration. Throw out routines and we have what we are lumbered with in our hospitals today: old people dying of dehydration, old people lying in their own excrement, old people with bedsores, old people who are ignored and abandoned, perhaps still clutching their own, little used, "person centred care plan".

Geriatrics. Like all terminology this word was evolving; some wards insisted on no longer calling the experience "geriatrics" but "psycho-geriatrics", the added word bringing an implication not just of "mental" to the phrase, but of increased importance. Both words should imply the study and care of older people. Obviously the latter implies a combination of the study of older people and of mental illness in old age. Within just a few years the term "geriatrics" was abruptly discarded, to be renamed E.M.I. (Elderly Mental Illness). From there it progressed to E.S.M.I. (Elderly Severe Mental Illness), the implication of the latter being dementia related. This terminology never sat comfortably: "I'm off to the 'Esmi Ward' was, to me, worse than the original term "geriatrics".

Psychiatry is littered with this abandoned terminology, dumped at the side of the so-called road to progress. Within the space of a few years terms are invented, marketed, used and abandoned with ridiculous rapidity. In the asylum the charge nurses just called it geriatrics. Semantics was of little interest to them. It never affected the care.

..........................

It was 7am on Ward 7, my first shift with Jack in charge. First shifts on a new ward were always that little bit different. This was to be no exception. None of the patients were up yet. Breakfast was at eight, so the day staff had little time to get things moving.

Clothes in those days, and for at least another decade, were communal. They were marked with "SP", (St. Paul's Hospital), and a ward number. It was the habit of most wards to "do the bundles" every afternoon. The nurses and nursing assistants would collect clothes for each of the patients, including underwear, from a linen store on each ward. These would then be "bundled" up and put next to the beds ready for the morning. Patients on these wards didn't have a choice of clothes. They wore what their bundle contained. It was one less thing to worry about.

Some staff, mostly female, worried whether the bundles would be appropriate for the coming day. A cold day would need warmer clothes. Bundling was a skilled occupation. What matched? What fitted? Did they wear tights? Did they wear a bra? If they did, how did a young male nurse put one on? I had only recently mastered how to take one off, thanks to a tolerant girlfriend. All these decisions made life difficult for the bundler.

I was not just an unskilled bundler; I was completely and utterly inept. Dresses were ill matched and ill fitted, trousers had no top buttons, and underpants were often confused with knickers. So when bundling was taking place I was generally bundled off to other tasks, bed-making perhaps, or false teeth cleaning, anything to get me out of the way. Other staff wanted clothes with a semblance of respectability and practicality. Being unconcerned about what my own clothes looked like, other peoples' clothes had little chance of fitting, let alone being practical. Were they cheap? Would they last? These were my only personal fashion criteria.

It was much later in my career that a female manager in the private sector commented on how terrible communal clothing must have been. "I couldn't stand the thought of wearing someone else's underwear, could you?" I'd never thought about this before, perhaps because, in the great scheme of things, it wouldn't really have bothered me! I might have drawn the line at pink knickers ......

Ward 7 had three Nightingale wards, thirty patients in total. Six staff was the full complement of hands available. So all the staff would pull their weight, including the charge nurse. Initially I was considered as an extra to numbers, but only for the first couple of weeks. After that I was a "proper" part of the staff numbers, so staff would expect me to "pull my weight".

But on my first morning I was still an extra. When the handover ended I joined Jack and Sally, a nursing assistant, in the smaller of the dormitories, which was for elderly male patients. I was directed to Eric, a gentleman who had been on the ward a considerable time, and who, unusually, had spent most of his adult life in the long stay wards. Now he suffered from dementia as well as schizophrenia and Parkinson's Disease, the reasons for his initial admission. Eric had been over six foot in his prime, but age had taken its toll on his stature as well as on his mind. He looked at me in a frozen, fixed stare, typical of Parkinson's sufferers. His legs were bent. His arms were on top of the bedclothes in a fixed pose, crossed in anticipation of death perhaps. He made no sound. Poor chap; it was my job to get him up.

"Just wash and get Eric up please. Me and Sally'll do the rest," said Jack hopefully. On the long stay wards the patients had sorted themselves out in the mornings, so I was completely bamboozled as to how to get an incapacitated patient up. Sally took me to the sluice and toilets. I mimicked her preparation: a trolley with a bowl of warm water, a white flannel (made from cut up towels), soap, and a safety razor (the cut-throat ones had, thankfully, been consigned to the dustbin of history). I returned to Eric.

After pulling the curtain round the bed I started by giving Eric a shave, a task I had done before, although on a corpse. He had no movement, being rigid and unable to turn his head. The shave was, at best, patchy, but at least he didn't look as if he'd been in a road traffic accident. The shaving finished I could now wash and dress Eric. Easier said than done. With his fixed limb and head presentations, his knees locked and his hands immovably set in a meerkat position, how could I remove his pyjamas? His legs and arms had no "give" to them?

"Jack!" I shouted through my curtain. No reply. Covering Eric with a towel I stepped out from behind the curtain. Two of the other beds were now empty. Where were Jack and Sally? I found them in the Day Room sitting their two patients up at a table, and giving them each a beaker of tea. "Can you give me a hand with Eric? I asked.

"Sure," said Jack, "you'll need help getting him into a chair."

We walked back to Eric. Jack swept the curtains aside. Eric sat there, rigid as ever, now slightly bloodied and showing dots of soap around his face.

"Hasn't he been washed?"

"No, I couldn't get his pyjamas off," I said forlornly.

I soon realised that there was no easy way of getting the pyjamas off someone with Parkinson's Disease, apart from brute force. Their arms and legs have no elasticity or free movement, no "bend", so gradual pressure had to be applied to each limb to move it to where it should be. This looked painful, but Jack did this with the least pressure required and with a confidence that got the job done. The creaking joints were very audible; I feared something would break. "Now get him washed," Jack instructed, Eric now naked, and with that left to help Sally.

Ten minutes later I had washed and dried Eric, but he was still lying there, naked, with a towel to cover his modesty.

"Jack!" I called, "Can you give me a hand?"

Again, no response.

Two more patients had been dressed and taken to the day room where Jack was sorting out a tray of blue pots, which contained all the patient's dentures soaking in "Steradent". Collecting one set of dentures he placed them into the mouth of a male patient. All wards still had their stories, probably true, of student nurses emptying all the dentures into a washing up bowl and cleaning them all together. The problem came when trying to sort out which dentures belonged to which mouth! It was the sort of mistake I could imagine myself making.

"Sorry to be a pest again Jack, but I'm stuck again with Eric."

"Is he washed?" asked Jack.

"Washed and ready to be dressed," I said confidently.

"Well, get him dressed then. What are you waiting for? Come on!"

Sheepishly I returned to Eric, deciding that the only way of doing this would be to get the appropriate clothes loosely fitting on his top half and loosely fitting round his lower legs, then to stand him up, pull the top set of clothes down and pull the bottom set of clothes up. Simple. Once done, put him in a wheelchair. But it all went wrong. I got the top half on, the bottom half on, but couldn't get him to stand up. So I had to leave him lying half dressed on the bed to ask again for help.

I found Sally starting to get cereal for her first patient. "Can you help me again with Eric?" I asked. With a sigh she wandered back up the ward to the dormitory. I explained where I had got to and that I needed to have help to stand him up and transfer him to a wheelchair.

"Can't you move him by yourself? I can!" She said reprovingly. I was beginning to understand that the work involved just getting on with things, finding ways round problems. I pulled the curtains back. Eric was there, but he had urinated. The stream of urine had covered all his lower garments.

"Why didn't you put the bottle under his penis? Might have saved you a bit of time!"

I removed Eric's soiled clothes and started the washing routine all over again. I made a new bundle with clothes that no one else wanted. They were hardly Eric's size and definitely not his colour. Eric had a late breakfast on that shift, that morning. I still had so much to learn. I needed to be more organised, more up to speed, before I could properly be counted as a part of the ward numbers.

Next time I'd choose someone else, someone easier than Eric.

..................................

In the late 70s there were few aids to continence, apart from catheterisation which was rarely used due to problems with fitting (very few staff were competent to do this procedure) and infection issues. "Inco-pads" were given out, but rarely of much use. These thick absorbent pads were stuffed through the legs between the skin and the underwear. However, they had no barrier, as modern nappies have, so the pads just filled up and once full slowly spread the urine everywhere.

The main method of dealing with incontinence was a regular, routine toileting regime. Almost all patients were taken to the toilet before breakfast, after breakfast, at 11, before lunch, after lunch, at 4pm, after tea, and before bed. Toileting rounds continued through the night. These fixed times were followed, come what may. Toileting routines were the main activity of each day. Indeed it was a real problem trying to squeeze anything else into a day, as one round of toileting almost ran into the next. Staff trying to take short cuts, or failing to really clean a patient after an "accident", were quickly brought to heel. "Keep 'em fed, watered and clean!" was the motto. And we did. It was drilled into us. Lots of things were worth arguing about; this wasn't. The toileting regime was sacrosanct. Within 10 years this system of routines had been junked. Nowadays we start to become almost immune to stories of huge pressure sores and of elderly people left in their own waste. During my training I never came across a bedsore. Patients were cleaned and toileted regularly. The regular change of scenery from day room to W.C. and back, combined with the patients being washed and dry clothes being put on, meant that bedsores were non-existent.

A charge nurse could cope with many accusations, but leaving patients unfed and wet was not an accusation that they would tolerate. In those days there was a lack of individuality and privacy. If done now it would certainly lead to accusations of abuse. But personally I would be quite prepared to surrender a bit of my dignity and a bit of my privacy in exchange for knowing that I was clean.

All patients were moved through to the male or female toilets for the routine. There were no hoists or aids to help with the moving, only a couple of wheelchairs. Patients were generally lifted by staff into a standing position, although some would just swing on the arms of the staff, their feet not even touching the ground, to be slowly lowered into a wheelchair, to be moved through to the toilets, where they would be man-handled off, undressed and put on a commode in the toilets. Usually just one member of staff undertook this "man-handling" of patients. It was almost "wimpish" and a wasteful use of staff to double up. There were, of course, no disabled toilets so patients who were only partially mobile, or completely immobile, had to use the commodes lining one side of the toilet area.

Although many patients had difficulty with walking, most seemed to have no problem at all with fidgeting and trying to get up. If they got up, they usually fell. The solution to this was a form of imprisonment on the commodes. Once a patient was sat on the commode their dress (if they were female) or shirt would be hooked onto the screws that were underneath the back of the toilet pan holding the seat to the base. This "hooking on" was key to patients not getting up and falling. They were only "un-hooked" once they had "performed".

"Have you hooked Eric on?" would be asked of me as I checked if he'd performed. "If you have, can you come and help me hook Tom on." Each patient was checked and, once they had "done their business", they were "unhooked", washed, clean clothes put on (not their own, of course, but clean and dry) and moved back to the Day Room.

We hear that elderly patients today are not regularly taken to the toilet, the reason given, "low staff numbers". But the staffing numbers today are double what they were then. The problem seems to stem partly from issues around "Person Centred Care", where each patient has a personal routine, but whole ward routines are non-existent. Nowadays there is also the problem around the machinery for moving patients. Patients are no longer allowed to be "lifted", for fear of nurses suing because of back injuries. But hoists and incontinence aids, far from improving care, seem to have conspired to decrease patient care, resulting in reduced cleanliness and increased pressure sores. The machinery is just too complicated to work. It is just not practical.

But the primary reason for this collapse in hygiene, with the concomitant rise in pressure sores, seems to be staff not wanting to be troubled by the baseness of such a procedure. They are too proud. An increase in wound damage and pressure sores is the sorry result.

It is now a rule that a nurse must have a Masters Degree before they can reach the position of a charge nurse or sister. This professionalism of nurses has led to many believing that they are too important to undertake basic care routines. They prefer to be close to the computers and Doctors, rather than sullying themselves in the more earthy side of nursing.

When patients were in open wards, open for all to see, ordered care and compassion was required. Visibility, just as much as morality, was the driving force behind such care and compassion. Nowadays patients are "Service Users", not patients. Nurses are required to care for patients. Are they required to give as much care to "service users"? Now that patients are hidden away in single rooms, who is to see? Now there aren't toileting routines, who is to notice if they have been incontinent? Have we progressed or regressed from regimented structures?

Jack, like all the charge nurses I worked with during my various geriatric experiences, was totally involved in the toileting regime. Although he did much of the paperwork and coped with management, when the time came round for toileting he was up on his feet, doing the same "menial" work as all the others. Find a ward manager today that does this. You'll have your work cut out. They're too busy with "other things".

In the late 70s, if you didn't do "earthy", if you were too proud to wipe bottoms, then you didn't do geriatrics. So nursing was not for you.

# CHAPTER SEVENTEEN

A few weeks after my arrival on Ward 7 Percy came to be admitted. Everyone knew Percy, a regular attendee. Even I knew Percy. He'd been with Jack that first day in the long corridor. Staff were delighted to see him, although he was subdued and withdrawn, giving little information about his condition. It was his fourth admission in the two years, so the admission procedure was notable for its brevity. Barbara, our psychiatrist, saw him within an hour of his arrival.

Small, bald, with sharp features, Percy was a person who'd go unnoticed in a crowd. But then Percy would never be in a crowd. Percy, a reluctant loner, was unassuming, quietly spoken and not an initiator of friendships or conversation. He dressed, always, in a sports coat, plain shirt and tie, grey trousers and from a distance he would look smart. Close up it was very apparent that the clothes were old and the tie frayed. He had little money, but just scraped by, too proud to ask for help, too proud to receive any state help, living off a small pension. There were no savings.

Barbara completed the medical. She'd known Percy for years, watching his admissions, seeing him in outpatients and even gaining a rudimentary knowledge of his interests. Un-flappable, Barbara was a rare psychiatrist in not being an empire builder as so many of the Ivan-the-Terrible psychiatrists were. As a female on the medical side she had coped with the bravado and over-confidence of these other psychiatrists, hearing, seeing but not joining in. She was there to do the job, but without searching for, or needing the kudos. She was, quite simply, safe to work with.

Percy joined the other patients in the day room, settling in a corner, away from noise. He looked downcast, but as I came to know him better, I realised that this was his usual appearance. Whereas almost all the patients were toileted, Percy "sorted himself out". This, to me, was quite novel. After tea I wandered over to chat with him, introducing myself to him again. He remembered me, or so he said. I asked him about why he'd come in. "They wanted me in," was all he said, looking away as soon as he'd answered. Going back to his notes I found that he came in when his mood slumped, that when this happened he ceased looking after himself and would revert to his bed, until rescued by the community psychiatric nurse.

Percy suffered from recurrent clinical depression. For some people depressions were isolated incidents, but for others the depression was a recurring nightmare, a visitation of total doom and despondency, which seemed to have no escape route. In the 1970s depressions were defined as either reactive (as a reaction to a situation) or endogenous (a depression with no known cause). As so often, the fashion changed in the terminology used. Reactive depressions changed to exogenous and then to adjustment disorders. It's interesting that the term endogenous depression, where there is no known cause, has not changed.

As my clinical knowledge expanded, I became less interested in whether there was, or wasn't, an obvious cause. The despondent feelings were the same. Some professionals appeared to be desperate to find causes, working their way methodically through a life history to find an episode that, they felt, was the root cause. I came to believe that my role was to identify a clinical depression and treat the symptoms. Once treated the patient could discuss other issues at will, which they couldn't if they were depressed.

Percy was my first experience of trying to understand this "mood disorder", as we were taught to think of it. The prevalent aspect of the depression, for Percy, was change: change in sleeping habits, change in appetite, change in concentration, change in interests, change in contact with people, change in outlook, change in motivation and drive. On top of all this, Percy suffered from a perpetual low mood. He came in principally to be cared for whilst his medication was adjusted. At the same time his admission gave him some real contact with people. He was pleased to be there. It was somewhere he felt safe.

As he mentally progressed I saw in him a very gentle and thoughtful individual. He became a chap who all staff wanted to spend a bit of time with, chatting about the TV, the food, where he lived, what he liked. Given the severity of the dementia with ninety per cent of our patients, it was just great having a patient who genuinely seemed interested in what was going on and who we were. He came to know us, as we came to know him. Much of the work on Ward 7 was repetitive and backbreaking. A diversion was a welcome relief. Two weeks after being admitted he was back to his bungalow. He'd return, in time, but he was always a welcome breath of fresh air.

..............................

The position of charge nurse was a position in the ward. It was not an intermediary between the ward and the office. The charge nurse or sister was an "us"; the nursing officers and administrators were a "them".

This was vividly illustrated one afternoon when Mr. Burridge, the senior nursing officer, was "acting down" for the nursing officer, and decided to pay Ward 7 a visit. Jack was on duty, and Mr. Burridge was always something of a red rag to a bull for Jack. Mr. Burridge, and all nursing officers liked to be formally addressed, first names weren't used, had the habit of only wanting to hear good news, tending to ignore negative comments. He disliked confrontation, but was generally an unloved character paying only cursory attention to his wards. Therefore he must have shuddered as he approached Ward 7. Although he saw me first, feeding a patient with a beaker of tea, he then spotted Jack. It was too late to retreat. Jack had been in the ward office, but was on his feet to begin his objections as Mr. Burridge walked in. Acknowledging Jack he raised his right hand in a half wave. "Hello Jack. Everything alright?"

It was the wrong question to ask Jack, who had already risen from his chair and was now standing in the doorway, in a confrontational posture. "No, Mr. Burridge! We are one staff member down. We are trying to maintain care without the minimum staffing needed."

"Oh," said Mr. Burridge. "Well, they all look very well cared for. Jolly good. So...." A long pause as he tried to think how to escape. "So.....everything alright then?" With that he turned but Jack was too quick for him.

"No Mr. Burridge! Things are NOT all right! Things are far from all right! We are short of staff and getting no help from you and your office."

"Right oh," Mr. Burridge maintained his usual tone, trying to avoid this confrontation. "Well, nice to see you all. Glad to see you're alright then." With that he started to stride up the corridor, dashing for safety. But, like a gillie after a wounded deer, Jack wanted one last shot.

"As I've said before, Mr. Burridge, no we are not alright! We are short of staff and you've done nothing to help!" Mr. Burridge must have only heard the beginning of this as, by that time, he was turning the corner into the main corridor. I never saw him on Ward 7 again.

Jack set the tone. Patients were patients. As they were patients, then it was the nurse's duty to care. From Jack's perspective, nursing officers were the facilitators of this care. For Jack, the nursing officers failed in their care. Hence the confrontations. Jack would never let them get away with it.

........................

Geriatrics was a hard, physically hard, business. Everyone suffered from bad backs, exhaustion and fear that they were being left on the back burner of professional development. To a student nurse it all seemed so routine orientated - the routines were so time-consuming. A meal in Ward 7 started when the patients were all sitting waiting. What were they waiting for? Most of them didn't really know. The meal ended, not when the patients had been fed and watered, with fragments of food splattered everywhere, being trodden into the carpeting as the staff went about their business, but ended only when the patients had been toileted and changed. It could be a heart-breaking job. Toileting meant a complete wash, change and all clean clothes for a patient. It was so demoralising to return a patient to the day room only to discover that they had been incontinent in the wheelchair on the way back, leaving a fluid trail running in a wobbly line along the corridor. Time to start again. The meal ended only when the patients were clean, the floor was clean and the tables cleared away. In reality the end of one routine was just the start of the next. For staff the routines never ended. For us the "end" only came when it was time for knocking off.

Very occasionally, there was a moment of light relief. These moments were treasured, retold, expanded on. They were memories that stuck. These brief periods of laughter were the interesting icing on a stale cake.

Jack was on duty for an afternoon shift. Sally, the staff nurse who usually worked with him, was on a long day – from 7 in the morning till 8 at night – so was becoming frazzled. The morning had been particularly bad due to Gerald, an ambulant patient with dementia, having an unexpected bout of diarrhoea. Usually Gerald was one of the very few who were able to sort out their own toileting. However, the ferocity of the diarrhoea had been too much even for him. Sally had changed and washed him on three occasions. Ward 7 was fast running out of clean clothes from the ward stock.

Jack suggested that Trudy, a nursing assistant, and I went for a break together before "doing" tea for the patients. We had been allocated the early break. Half the patients had been toileted. Jack and Sally were going to toilet the second half, then start the patients' tea and take their break when we returned.

Trudy and I sloped off to the canteen for tea, expecting and receiving the dried up left-overs from lunch, served without finesse by one moody catering assistant. Half and hour later we returned to the ward, hardly refreshed, but at least with something in our stomachs, to work the last four hours of the shift.

Patients' teatime was underway. Jack and Sally were ready for their break. Jack was serving from the "hot trolley", a large wheeled metal servery. Sally was feeding patients, waiting to hand me the spoon for the patient she was looking after.

As I pulled on my white coat Jack motioned to me. "We've fed these, but haven't done their pudding. Those patients," he pointed to a group in one corner, "still need feeding. All of them need to be changed after tea into their pyjamas and dressing gowns. Before we go, can you just check the toilets to make sure you've got enough nightclothes? Then we can go to our tea. I'll do the medication when I get back."

I strolled through to the toilets to check on the available clothes, always a constant worry. Would there be sufficient for the change after tea? As I entered the male toilet area, I was stunned by what I saw. Across the floor, by the rows of washbasins, around the commodes, an explosion of excrement covered the whole area. Lumps here and there, but mostly oozing dollops of it. I stood aghast, staring at the unholy mess, a scene of light brown slurry. But something wasn't quite right. What? I despaired. Returning to the day room I found Jack and Sally eager to go for their tea.

"Has Gerald been down here?"

"Why?" said Jack, impatient to get off.

"The floor's covered. Surely you noticed. Gerald must have been covered in it! Come and see."

Jack stopped. "Hang on Sally, there's a bit of a problem." They followed me into the male toilet. Trudy was behind. All three stood, gazing at the mess. Each looked to another for an answer.

Sally broke the silence. "I never actually saw Gerald come through here. Did you see him Jack?"

Jack thought for a moment. "No, I don't think I saw him come up to the toilets. Maybe it wasn't Gerald." He stared at the excrement. Again there was silence.

Eventually Jack warily approached the closest revolting sludge and crouched down. To our utter amazement he scooped up a handful of the diarrhoea and studied it carefully, before licking and then swallowing it. A stunned silence.

We stood open mouthed. Putting his hand in front of his mouth he sniffed his breath. "Yes, that's Gerald's." He walked out.

Trudy and I gagged.

Sally followed Jack, without a word. Jack stopped off to wash his hands. I waited, astonished, trying to grasp what I'd just seen.

Then Sally creased up. Trudy and I knew we'd been "had".

The kitchen had supplied powdered puddings for tea. Tonight's pudding had been toffee mousse, a disgusting watery mixture of toffee-flavoured granules, bulking agents and egg powder. It was badly digested by our patients on the past occasions of it's presence on the menu, and Jack had made complaints to the kitchens about its lack of suitability. But it was cheap, so had made yet another sorry appearance. Jack had set the whole thing up, splattering the mousse around the toilets. It was only now that I realised what was wrong: there was no smell, no smell of diarrhoea!

As Jack and Sally giggled their way up the corridor, to share the joke with others in the cafeteria, I shouted, "but when I got here Gerald was just coming out of the toilets! Are you sure he didn't add anything?" It was a valiant effort to pass the joke back, but in reality we knew the joke was on us.

It was one of the very few times I saw such laughter on the ward. The story was told again and again and again. It wasn't that it was an unhappy ward, but the work meant that it was always a hard grind.

A minor childish episode, a brief interlude from the routines, made the repetitive work slightly less intolerable.

# CHAPTER EIGHTEEN

Deaths on Ward 7 occurred in the best viewing position. Passing on, although not a regular spectator event, was at least carried out in the most visible place, the bed by the office window. If I'm ever asked if I want a bed by the window, I shall refuse, unless, that is, I'm dying. That bed position is, to me, where people are expected to shuffle off their mortal coil. When I am ready for death then I'll happily be window bound. I should have a better chance of having some degree of personal care. Don't put me in a side room. That is the place to die alone, unseen, forgotten.

The nurses office on Ward 7, although on the main corridor, had a large window that overlooked one of the main wards. There was a progression of status in who slept where, with patients moving up the ward, towards the window as they became frailer and sicker. Betty had been on the ward for many months, but for the past three weeks she had resided in a bed behind the window, allowing her the status of being deemed the poorliest on the ward. There was logic behind this. The sickest needed to be where they could be seen at all times and, given the through traffic of professionals who visited Ward 7, there was never any doubt that this bed position was the most viewed. Any failure of good care would be immediately spotted.

Diagnosed on admission with dementia, as time progressed it became evident that Betty was now suffering from terminal cancer. The dual diagnoses ruled out, for her, the need for intrusive investigation. What type of cancer was it? By the time it was diagnosed, it had metastasised through her body. She was riddled with it. Rightly, in my opinion, the location of the primary cancer was not a significant concern. The doctors and family knew she was terminally ill, so she should be treated kindly and lovingly, without too much "prodding around". Now she was emaciated, mute and, even with her eyes open, did not seem aware of what was going on around her. Her frailty was very evident for all to see. She had not been able to bear her own weight for as long as she'd been on the ward and her legs and arms had become twisted and bent. Her knees, particularly, had contracted, now needing cushions underneath them for support.

Although the doctors saw her daily, she had declined still further, a little bag of sorry bones barely hidden by her stretched almost luminescent skin. She lay with four pillows under her shoulders and head to prop her up, to lessen the risk of a chest infection. Her white hair was now just a few sorry strands. Around her front she always had a woolly blanket. Her gnarled hands would gently fiddle with this blanket throughout the day, giving some form of tactile comfort.

Nowadays a patient in this condition, immobile, frail, taking only minimal nutrition and fluids, would be on an "airwave" mattress, with a set of inflatable cells, much like a Lilo, which fill and deflate from a computer, to stop pressure damage; but this machine it also stops the need for comfort, support, love and attention. Betty didn't need this equipment to help her. She was supported, washed, and comforted by the staff. The airwave mattress, in comparison, is a useless comforter.

At some point the doctors decided to start her on morphine injections. It was said that this was to deal with any pain she was having, although there was an unspoken understanding that this would also allow her to slip away rather sooner.

Jack knew about my saga of my injections fiasco and so, one morning around coffee time, he suggested that I might give Betty her morphine injection. Morphine injections were given, like the depot injections, into the muscle. Unlike depot injections, morphine was a simple water based injection and so was considered to be easier to administer. It would, he suggested, boast my "confidence with the needle". Jack also felt that student nurses should be exposed to difficult situations, not protected from them.

I drew up the injection and went with Jack to Betty's bedside. Talking to her about what we were about to do, I pulled back the bedclothes. I rolled her legs away from me, exposing her thigh. Where does one find muscle in a lady who was no more than a bag of bones? Jack bunched together some skin in his fist, creating a small area of tissue. "Hold it like this, then insert the needle slowly, so as not to hit the bone."

Trying to hold the syringe, the swab, and a fistful of skin wasn't easy. However, I was determined not to make the mistake of tapping the skin with the needle. I knew it needed some significant pressure to enter the skin. I pushed the needle in firmly, immediately hitting the bone. The jarring went up through my arm; I can still feel this as I write. The blood drained from my face but I pressed the plunger home and withdrew the needle, knowing that I would have created a slight barb, but also knowing that there was nothing I could do about it now.

Betty died half an hour later. The curtains were then drawn around her bed. I like to think that she died free from pain, but worried for a considerable time about whether my clumsy, but well meant injection, had created more pain or less.

The doctor came to pronounce death and Sarah and myself completed the last offices, the preparation of the body after death. Once completed, I was told to contact Fred, the porter, to take Betty to the mortuary. It was one o'clock when I phoned the switchboard for Fred. The operator told me she'd contact him. Jack warned me that Fred would be in the Social Club.

Twenty minutes later Fred arrived on the ward. He was a long stay fixture in the asylum, having been employed there since he was eighteen. Now large in every way, perhaps 20 stone, he always had a fag hanging out of the corner of his mouth. I knew Fred as he was regularly, very regularly, "down the Social Club". He knew all the patients by name; they seemed more comfortable chatting to him than to me. Fred was one of those people who never seemed to smile; a frown perpetually on his face, yet he always seemed to radiate happiness. His wit was dry; his language coarse, but he never spoke ill of staff or patients - holding his venom back for senior management. At ease with himself, everyone was at ease with him. Wonderful, chatty and natural with the patients, he gave them his time, as well as his conversation, when others couldn't be bothered. When he came to the ward he'd wander round the day room indulging in gentle banter with the elderly people there. He had an easy manner that they all responded to.

"Hi Stuart, didn't see you round the Club last night. Were you well?"

"Other things on." In truth I still had been suffering a hangover from the night before.

"So, where is she?" he asked.

Taking him through to the ward and I pulled aside the curtains. As he bent over to look at her I was aware that he stank of whisky. He had obviously been on his lunchtime session when called.

"I'll bring the wagon in a while," he said, looking at the corpse, "but she'll never fit in the coffin with those knees. The lid'll never close." He measured the height of the knees with his eyes. "No, the undertakers won't get the lid of the coffin down. We'll have to break 'em. More booze. That's what I need." Then he was gone, back to the Club for some more "Dutch Courage", or should that be "Scotch courage". Did I sign up as a student nurse to break the legs of a corpse? My job description had been vague, but.....

A couple of hours later Fred, with bloodshot eyes, and reeking of whisky, returned with a metal trolley, known as the "blood wagon". This was a trolley with a lift up lid in which all bodies were transferred to the mortuary. Everyone understood exactly what the blood wagon was about, despite the fact that it was covered with a mauve cloth, in a feeble attempt to hide its dread purpose. The blood wagon was the obvious sign that the grim reaper had been doing his rounds.

"Hold the shoulders down while I push the legs down. They should break easy," Fred said, sensing my squeamishness. Tentatively I held her shoulders, unaware of what was about to happen. Fred suddenly slammed his weight on Betty's knees, thrusting them down. Betty, or should I say the corpse, immediately sat up, breaking free from my feeble grip. Fred relaxed and the corpse fell back, the knees returning to their original position. Getting into a better position above the corpse Fred threw all his weight down onto the knees again. Despite my desperate attempt to keep them flat to the bed, the shoulders and head sat up again. Each subsequent attempt by Fred to thrust down on the knees brought Betty back to an upright position with her head lolling forward. At each attempt there was a terrible creaking of joints, accompanied by various unpleasant gurgling sounds from the corpse, but there was no snapping of bones. This was repeated about a dozen times, each time with the same outcome. Betty had become a nodding donkey. Her knees, locked in position, were just not going to break.

Fred stood back, wiping the sweat from his brow. "Beds are too bloody soft...Need something firmer. Just have to take 'er over to the mortuary. I'll do it there. With a stone slab under 'er, they'll crack."

This was a relief. I didn't really want anything more to do with this roughing up of a corpse.

Betty was placed in the "blood wagon" as carefully as her contorted limbs would allow. Together we took her outside and round the ring road to the mortuary. Bodies were always taken outside; the only reason I could ever find for this was that it was supposed to be bad luck if bodies were transported indoors.

Leaving the ward from the back of the asylum we passed Percy sitting on a bench outside the door. As we pushed the wagon down the ramp his eyes lifted. He stood, bowed his head, watched the wagon pass with lowered head, and then resumed his position on the bench, staring at the cricket field. He was simply a gentleman. It was so unusual to find someone with such fine manners in this very odd place.

As we passed Ward 9, another long stay male ward, one of the patients, who I knew slightly, was going through a refuse bin looking for fag ends. He was almost upended, stretching deep into the bin to snatch at the fag ends buried at the bottom. Debris from his search was scattered all around. Hunting for fag ends was a serious business. As he returned to a standing position he glanced the wagon.

"Watcha' Fred. Another one gone?"

"Yeah. Nothing to worry about," replied Fred.

"Which ward?" the fag hunter asked.

"Ward 7."

"Bloke or woman?"

"A bloke," responded Fred quickly, continuing to push the gurney towards the mortuary.

I nudged Fred, "God! You must have put away a fair amount of booze today. It's a woman you pillock! You've just spent twenty minutes trying to break her bloody legs."

Fred stopped, turned me towards him and whispered, "Never tell 'im it's a woman. If 'e knows there's a woman in there, 'e'll get into the mortuary and shag 'er! Done it before – but 'e'll never bother if it's a man."

The asylum did this to me. It always came up with surprises and shocks.

Fred, drunk though he was, the inveterate keeper of morals in this unbelievable place!

# CHAPTER NINETEEN

Nowadays elderly people suffering from dementia requiring admission will tend to be admitted, not to a hospital, but to a private care home. Those with other psychiatric illnesses requiring admission, tend to go to the acute units. But back in the 1970s almost anybody over 65 requiring admission, with a suspected psychiatric diagnosis, would be placed in the geriatric wards of the asylum. So older people with psychoses, depressions and various other illnesses would come through the geriatric wards of St. Paul's. This led to a bizarre mix of the confused, the disturbed, the depressed and the anxious, though the confused were by far the largest group.

Jeffrey was a new admission into Ward 7. Arriving early for a shift I saw the name. A new name was always of great interest to me, so I decided to meet him. In a side room sat a smart gentleman of around 70, wearing a bright woollen cardigan and quietly reading a book, an activity that I rarely saw in the geriatric wards. Along with Percy, that meant there were now two relatively smart patients, both actually wearing their own clothes. A rarity on Ward 7!

He greeted me with a cheery "hello." I introduced myself. He was reading an Alistair MacLean book and was obviously able to concentrate fully on it. Again, a novelty. He told me he lived in the local village, living alone since he had divorced his wife some years previously. He was ordered in his thinking and appropriate in everything we discussed. My thoughts were running wild. Why had he been admitted?

At handover, I was all ears. Jeffrey had come in the previous day, brought by the police. Two days previously he had knocked on his neighbour's door, clutching a "Stanley" knife. As the door opened he had launched himself at the startled middle-aged man, slashing at him with the knife, causing extensive chest and arm wounds. Witnesses to the attack bravely went to the man's aid. Jeffrey was quickly overpowered and removed to the Police Station, where he was assessed by the police surgeon and sent to our ward for further assessment.

Mostly Jeffrey just sat and read in his room, although he was always pleased when staff dropped in to check on him. It was an excuse for a chat and intelligent company, both for him and us. It was always refreshing to have a patient on the ward to talk to at a level beyond the daily routine.

However, a few days after his arrival, I overstepped the mark, straying into areas that I had no knowledge of, or ability to cope with.

Having discussed the book and the weather I tried to open a new avenue of discussion.

"Tell me about where you live."

"In an old semi. Bought after my divorce. Nice garden. All modernised. Used to love it."

"Used to? It sounds great. Have you friends in the area?"

"I've got lots of friends." A short pause. "My son and daughter come and see me regularly. All the way from Ipswich."

"So why've you've gone off it? The house I mean." I enquired.

"It'd be lovely, really lovely, if it wasn't for the bloke next door."

"What's wrong with him?" I asked, in my innocence.

"I discovered he'd been getting into my loft. It's one of those lofts where there's just a breezeblock wall. When I went up there, to sort out the aerial, some of these blocks were gone, between my loft and his. I looked through the gap and saw some wires and things close to the hole. I knew..... HE'D been setting up equipment, equipment to spy on me. I knew. He'd started to interfere with the electricity in my house. This equipment.... It was starting to change my brain waves, to hurt my head, to alter what I was thinking. It was making me do things that he wanted. If I didn't do these things he'd turn up the power of his equipment, causing me pain, headaches, a knocking feeling in my brain." He stopped, going into a thoughtful mode.

This was reminiscent of the James Tilly Matthews "Air Loom Gang" delusions.

"Did the equipment ever actually cause you any pain?" I asked.

"Yeah. More and more pain. There was nothing I could do. It altered my thinking, affected my brain. He had electrical control over the whole of my house. It all came through that hole in the loft. It was such a nice house, so comfortable and safe. Then he moved in. The pain started.... Now I dread it "

"What do you think he wanted from you?"

"He never made it clear. It was all about controlling me. Probably he would have told me, in time. First he had to be certain he'd got his power over me."

I tried one more tack. "Don't you think that you might have misunderstood what you saw and felt? You might have just misread the situation. He might not be a bad person at all. There may be other explanations."

There was a long silence.

Suddenly he stood up, eyes blazing and started to smash at the walls and the doors with his bare fists. The attack wasn't against me. It was blind frustration at my failure to understand his plight. He's experienced it; he'd thought it through; he'd lived it! Why couldn't I understand? Was I on the neighbour's side? In his fury he continued to savagely kick the walls and door, insensitive to the state of his bloodied knuckles.

I beat a hasty retreat. Once I was out of the way Jeffrey quickly settled down. I came to realise that questioning a patient was a skilled art, with dire consequences if one overstepped the mark. I tried not to overstep the mark again, especially with Jeffrey. As long as the question of the neighbour wasn't raised, then he was fine.

He was initially given a diagnosis of paraphrenia, a type of older age schizophrenia, which in the 70s was a diagnosis commonly used to describe isolated delusional states in older people. The diagnosis of paraphrenia was a fading fashion then. Today it is completely out of fashion.

Jeffrey attended court, convinced of his innocence. He merely stated that the action he had taken that day had been in self-defense. He was found to be of unsound mind due to a severe psychiatric condition. He could be discharged as long as he agreed to live elsewhere and remain under a psychiatrist's care.

This decision just added to Jeffrey's feelings of persecution. Why was he in court anyway? He'd done nothing wrong!

However, while the professionals argued, and Jeffrey protested, he was found to have an inoperable brain tumour – the real cause of his delusion and his pain. He died in the general hospital some months later.

His neighbour would have to live with the scars of this extremely violent, yet random attack.

This was one of those terrible situations where there had been no obvious threat, until the incident had occurred. Years later, in New Zealand, I came across a similar incident where a patient I was visiting told me that he had, just hours previously, been to visit his neighbour. He'd knocked on the door, with a loaded shotgun at the ready, to shoot him. The neighbour happened to be out so my patient had simply returned home and put the gun away. Luck had held that day in New Zealand; luck hadn't held for Jeffrey's neighbour.

..........................

The most common diagnosis on the geriatric wards was dementia. The care given to most dementia sufferers was routine toileting, routine cleaning, routine feeding and routine changing. However, some patients such as Eric who I'd struggled to get up on that first day, arrived in our geriatric ward as a progression, or perhaps an inverted promotion, from the long-stay wards. Eric had moved to Ward 7 as a result of a combination of Parkinson's Disease and "going off his feet". But sometimes patients were admitted to us because of concerns that their age made it difficult for them to cope with the rough and tumble of the long stay wards.

Donald was a legend of the asylum. The first thing you noticed was his walk. He walked hunched forwards with short rapid steps. He seemed always to be on the point of falling, though he rarely did. He wore an old, oversized sports coat, which hung from his bent shoulders like a cloak. The first view of Donald was always the top of his bald head, which seemed to arrive long before his body. His head would peer through a door, glance both ways, and then disappear.

He never spoke, though a few noises, a cross between "urgh" and "argh", emerged if there was something that altered or upset his very fixed routines. He was fixed about where he sat, where he walked, what he ate for breakfast, when he washed. Everything was fixed. If someone took his chair the "urgh, argh" noises started, getting louder until something changed so that he could resume his usual routine.

Now in his late 70s, Donald had been admitted when he was just sixteen. His admission diagnosis, still in his medical notes stored in the ward office, told me that he had the original diagnosis of "intellectual insanity". He had been in the asylum ever since. He had been one of the nomads, exploring all areas of the asylum, fighting fiercely for his own corner and living an odd life even for this very odd place. Everyone knew Donald.

Although I regularly spoke to Donald, a "hello" or "thank you", he never uttered anything in reply. The older staff remembered a time when he would mutter monosyllables, though this had been many years earlier. I first noticed him sitting in front of the TV blocking anyone else's view. When I say he was sitting in front of the TV, I really mean "in front of..." He sat on a stool with his nose just touching the centre of the screen. His right hand held the glass bottom of a milk bottle, with a piece of wire wrapped around it, through which he stared, one-eyed, at the screen. With this dilapidated monocle, he peered at the middle of the screen, then slowing sliding his nose to a corner, then back to the middle, then to another corner.

This thorough inspection continued until all four corners and the centre had been examined. I hadn't realised this was part of Donald's fixed routine so, rashly, I moved to him and tapped him on the shoulder, intending just to ask his to move so others could see the screen. The shoulder tap was enough for a response. Donald stood up – a long way up. I'd never seen him standing fully upright before. I found myself looking up, a long way up, as he started to shout "aargh, aargh," again and again, louder and louder.. His mouth was wide, his eyes staring. What to do? I wondered.

"Leave Donald alone," shouted Jack from the office. "He'll move in a minute. He checks the TV like this every so often. There, he's off now." Donald was on the move again.

I grew used to Donald and his routines. Never touch him was the rule. Interference in his routines led to him becoming noisy, a sign possibly of his fear. As I watched he would perform the same routine with other items in the ward: pictures in the corridor, his food, books and notices. The examination was always thorough; it was enough to check that everything was as he felt it should be in his very ordered world.

Jack told me about Donald. "I remember him when I first started. He was already a long stay fixture then. He worked in the boiler department, shoveling coal into the boilers. He could fill a large barrow full, and I mean full, of coal. Then he'd push it through to the furnace on his own. Mostly it needed two patients to do this. He'd then empty the barrow into the furnace before starting again. He did this all his working life, apart from Saturdays and Sundays, when staff would be there in enough numbers to do it without him."

"Didn't he ever ask to do something else?"

"This wasn't a work scheme. This was an asylum in the old days. It was his job. It was always his job. It never changed. Why would it?"

"But he did get weekends off?" I asked, as though this was a privilege. Donald's net pay over a week of this backbreaking work would be just a few pennies.

"Didn't need him at weekends," said Jack. "Staff always want to work week-ends for the weekend rate, so he never had a chance at weekend work."

"Just love his monocle," I said, changing the subject. "Never seen one before."

"He's taken to using a monocle since struggling to make normal spectacles. He used to make "specs" from two milk bottle bottoms, connected usually with pipe cleaner wire. Of course he refused to see an optician. His eyesight was better then, a lot better. He got by with his home-made specs."

In 1981 Donald and another patient were formally presented with commemorative medals for 65 years of "service" to the hospital. Although not present at the ceremony, I cannot imagine them taking the risk of hanging the medal around Donald's lowered neck, for fear of Donald's unpredictable response!

Jack chatted on about what he knew of Donald. "He was a swimmer, you know."

I couldn't imagine Donald swimming. It was so incongruous. Where had he learned to swim? It was yet another snippet of Donald's life that would never get an explanation. "Have you seen him swim?" I asked, thinking this may be an "old wives tale".

"Oh yeah. Used to go to the seaside every year. Used to take about eight of them in the old coach. When we got there Donald would wander off down to the sea. He never waited for the thermos flasks to be brought out for a cuppa; he just wandered off. I'd watch him strip down to his underpants, leave his clothes on the high tide line and then stride off into the sea. When he was about waist high he'd plunge forward and swim out."

"Didn't anyone go with him?"

"He wouldn't have anyone with him, he's a loner; always has been, always will be."

"So," I persevered, "how long did he stay out there?"

"For as long as we stayed. We'd look up and see his head, way out at sea, bobbing up and down. Usually stayed a couple of hours. All this time he'd be out at sea. He'd have been frozen. Eventually he must have seen the rest of us start to pack up. Then he'd swim back, reach his clothes, dry himself with a scraggy towel he'd put in his jacket pocket, pull off his now drenched pants and dress again. Donald wasn't one for modesty.

He'd then clamber onto the bus. Donald's a funny chap. No one's ever really to get to know him."

Donald was the Captain Webb of St. Paul's. Who'd have thought it?

# CHAPTER TWENTY

Acute psychiatry can be defined as 'sharp', the implication being "quick in and out". Almost all younger nurses wanted to work in this dynamic field. It was the vibrant end of the psychiatric scale, high profile, varied patients, a sense of patients actually going home, actually getting better. Conferences, academic papers, new ideas, that was what acute psychiatry was all about. Long stay and geriatric "specialties" were tired old backwaters. Acute psychiatry would be where the patients went home, perhaps leaving a bunch of flowers for the staff, heartfelt thanks for all their hard work in the transition from acute illness to thriving well-being.

How naïve could I be?

I was to do my acute experience on Ward 24, which, although part of St. Paul's Hospital, was about a mile up the road, half way between the asylum and the Nurses Home. Ward 24 was a long way from immediate help if problems arose, and also a long way from the Social Club. There could be no link between handing in the day report and propping up the bar for the last two hours of the late shift.

A single story building, it was split along its length between female and male, linked, as always, by a long corridor. Each unit had a twenty bed Nightingale Ward, along with ten side rooms. The side rooms were used either as a privilege for good behaviour, or as secure and once lockable rooms, for more dangerous and violent behaviour. In the centre of Ward 24 were a dining room and occupational therapy room, where patients of both sexes could mix, if only briefly.

I was to work both ends of Ward 24, experiencing the male and female admission units. It was on Ward 24 that I met two of the most bizarre characters from my student days. They were both on duty for my first acute shift.

Hughie was the charge nurse for that first shift. Back at the Social Club Jack and Bob had filled me in about Hughie and some of his peculiarities. Hughie was unique in the hospital, being an "old lag", a term he approved of enormously, but unlike the others, Hughie neither drank, nor smoked, nor chased women. Also, unlike the other "Old Lags", he had never moved with the times. His parents had worked in the asylum and he had started as a student nurse around the same time as Jack. However he was not as bright as Jack and struggled to gain his qualification. But he was nothing if not determined so when he finally achieved the precious R.M.N. badge he started to climb the ladder of promotion. Despite being stuck in his old-fashioned ways, reluctant and possibly incapable of taking on new ideas, he slowly climbed the greasy pole. He never got his wallet out and so had the luxury, in a few years, of buying his house outright.

He became a charge nurse, though without the panache and good instincts of most of his comrades. He was the last of the old school to call all male student nurses "boy", his way of showing his innate superiority. Opinionated, loud and full of his own professional importance, he struggled to fit in. Unlike most of his peers, he was never able to think around complex issues, failing to grasp any of the greyer areas of psychiatry. To him every situation was a definite, even when he was proved wrong.

Always right, even when wrong, he was not an easy man to work for.

Hughie was a tennis player, occasionally joining us for our tennis matches. But he was always rather a strain, never quite in tune with our odd sense of humour. Winning was all-important to him. For the rest of us, winning was great, but the fun of the fight was even more important. A rising ball striking your opponent painfully was more of an accolade to be gloated over in the pub, than who had actually won. Even playing tennis Hughie insisted on calling me "boy". I remained a lower life form, whether in the ward or on the court. The progression from "boy" to "Stuart" only occurred on the day I qualified.

Staff loved to mimic Hughie behind his back. Any potential mimicry started with a grotesque parody of his large toothy grin, followed by a string of his bizarre and inane pearls of wisdom. It was the Hughie grin that I met on that first day on Ward 24. Hughie wore an immaculate white coat (washed by his wife each day) proudly displaying all his insignia of office. Fortunately he handed most of the responsibility for training me to a senior student nurse, Ron. Hughie always passed over teaching responsibilities to others on the feeble excuse that teaching students was really beneath him. Everyone knew that it was not just beneath him, but also beyond him. Most of my shifts would be with Hughie. This was not good, but Ron's presence made the shifts bearable. I would meet the other charge nurse, Kenny, but only rarely. After suffering under Hughie, Kenny was a joy to work with.

Ron was the archetypal left-wing communist agitator, with beard, jeans and unkempt hair to match. He wore a white coat, as we all did, but delighted in the fact that his was never sent for a wash.

He loved chaos, unorthodoxy and disarray. His knowledge and understanding were much greater than mine, with a flexible mind that could approach things in a different way from others. He had the knack of taking a subject and coming at it from an angle I would never have thought of. Modern in his thinking, he would stick by you when things went wrong. Although his views were modern, much of his behaviour fitted in well with the old lags. I remember a long discussion on diets with him over a few pints in the Social Club. He was so knowledgeable explaining the effects of differing foods and dietary patterns on behaviour, psychiatric conditions and life expectancy; I was so impressed by the breadth of his learning and the understanding. To me he was a perfect role model. Finally he expressed his own approach to diet: "Of course, I work on the theory that all one really needs is three pints of bitter a day and two vitamin tablets. You can live forever on a diet like that!" Sadly, shortly after completing his studies, Ron was admitted to an acute unit for alcoholism, which he battled with for many years.

Within a couple of shifts I started to see the variety of conditions in patients on the ward. They seemed so different from the patients I'd seen in my long stay and geriatric experiences. I shared this view with Ron, who thought about it for a while.

"In what way are they different?"

"Well," I was having to think on my feet, trying to compose a logical argument but aware that I was possibly digging myself into a large hole. "Most of these patients will get better, leave here and not return. So what we do here has a positive impact on their lives. But in long stay, the patients are there and they never change. And in geriatrics, we are there to care and support the patients knowing they will all die quite soon." I thought this was a pretty good stab at explaining the differences. I was quite proud of myself.

Ron lit another roll up cigarette. "Let's have a look at the list of whom we have in the ward at the moment," He picked up the ward clipboard and handed it to me. "How many of those do you think have been admitted more than twice?"

I scanned the list of thirty names. "Not sure. Two or three possibly?"

Ron took the clipboard back. "Of the names on here, half have been in three or more times. Of those remaining, more than half have been in here for more than six months. Most of the rest shouldn't even be here, referred by the courts for assessment, perhaps because they're violent, but without any real indication that they suffer a mental illness. In fact, as I scan the list, I can't see one of these patients being discharged and not returning within six months."

With this gloomy outlook, I asked him if he was ever positive about acute in-patient psychiatry.

"No. If someone gets in here they are well and truly stuffed. If they really need this level of hospitalisation, the chances are they'll always need it. There's a difference between acute psychiatry and the long-stay or geriatric wards. In those wards most of the patients are genuinely sick, or totally institutionalised, so it's our job to care for them as they decline and die." Ron took another drag of his cigarette, tapping the ash into the broken glass ashtray on the desk – broken when thrown a couple of weeks before. "But Ward 24 is different. About two-thirds of the patients are sick, chronically sick. They have to come in to be stabilised, usually given more medication, but once in here they become dependent on us. We discharge them, but for shorter and shorter periods. It's the revolving door syndrome again. And the other third, often drug addicts or, maybe, alcoholics, well, I don't know. Should they be here at all? What do we do for them? Where should they be? We probably do them more harm than good. It's a depressing place to work."

My student colleagues and I had been so excited by the chance to work on the acute wards. Bob and Jack had been less than enthusiastic; I was soon to see why. Acute in-patient work quickly lost its sparkle; there was little sense of job satisfaction. At least with long stay and geriatrics I could go home at the end of the shift feeling that I'd done something useful, that I had made a difference.

# CHAPTER TWENTY-ONE

John was a walking disaster. Usually sporting gauze dressings on his scarred face, as a result of trips and falls and cuts, he was a silent movie character in action. With his rapid walks, his erratic movement and his terrible capacity for being tragically accident-prone, he was a Keystone Cop character in reality, but without any sense of joy in the eyes of the beholder. As the mistakes, the clumsiness, the chaos continued, indeed grew worse as his heightened mood - his mania - took hold, so there increased in the staff a sense of wanting to wrap him in cotton wool, to protect him from himself. Anything to stop him being such a tragic clown. We never succeeded.

John and Peggy were regulars on Ward 24. For them Ward 24 was more of a home than their own home. It was definitely tidier than their own home, and the food was far better. Both had long-standing diagnoses of manic-depressive disorder, rarely under control. They had met and courted in St. Paul's when they were both in-patients and now had been married for more than fifteen years. Although both in their late forties, they looked more than sixty, their medication a catalyst for premature ageing. When I came across them John had been an in-patient on our male side for the previous few weeks and Peggy had just been discharged after four weeks on the female side. They were like the ornamental weather couple. When she came out, he went in, and vice versa. It was very rare for them both to be out, or in, at the same time. And yet, through all this, they remained besotted with each other.

John was small, slight and almost bald, a few strands of white hair left providing a slight covering. Sleeked down it partially succeeded, but he didn't seem to worry that, for most of the time, it fell on the opposite side of his head, resulting in a lop-sided thatch. His walk, like so many who had been on strong medication for so long, was odd. With long erratic jerky strides he moved, like a slouched Groucho Marx, surprisingly fast for someone who seemed to be in such poor condition.

His conversation was limited. With Peggy he communicated with a touch or a look and she could convey his needs to others. When he was on Ward 24 he would always be "high", gabbling interminably, what is called "pressured speech", typical of people with this disorder. He hardly ever slept, wandering clumsily around the house, when at home, or the ward when in (which was for a majority of the time). He would slouch purposely from one place to another, only to be distracted by the overwhelming need to move on to yet another place before reaching his first destination. This would be repeated again and again and again, all night. Yet Peggy remained loyal.

However, unlike some with manic depression (as it was called then, now it's called Bipolar Disorder), John was never happy when he was high. He became exhausted, fractious, frustrated and unaware of his deteriorating condition. He was prescribed more and more medication to stem the ever-ascending mood. There was often a feeling that if he got any higher he would eventually explode. During these periods Peggy would visit the ward on a daily basis, mostly sitting with us. She could no more keep up with the speed of his walk than she could with the speed of his interminable ramblings.

The office, as in most wards, had a window that looked out onto a four-bedded area known as the admissions ward. The nearest bed was always the one to watch. Anytime anyone went into the office they would automatically lift the curtain to check on the occupant of that bed. However Hughie, the charge nurse, was almost always sitting behind the desk, rearranging his office toys. When he was on duty staff spent little time there. The admissions ward was for patients who needed extra vigilance. John was in the first bed, nearest the window. He was there for a reason. Around each bed a curtain hung from a curtain track. This would be open at all times except when a patient was getting undressed. The patient in this closest bed needed the most observation. Being in that bed was the visible statement of their potential danger, to themselves or to others. This was John's bed.

A couple of weeks after I started, I went into the office to check the diary. As I reached for the diary, I heard a noise, a slight thump, nothing alarming but there was something different about it. My adrenaline surged. I flicked the curtain to check John's bed. Shit. My blood ran cold.

"Ron... Ron! Help!"

John had a rope round his neck. He was suspended between the curtain track and the floor, with the tip of one foot just touching the ground. The track had partially been torn from the ceiling by his jump from the bed, but remained fixed at other points. As I lifted John upwards to take the pressure off the rope, Ron grabbed the curtain track and ripped the whole system from the ceiling. Laying John on the bed, we removed the rope from around his neck.

John was shouting, "I'm sorry... I'm sorry... I'm sorry! I'm sorry!" again and again and again. He was crying, sobbing and shaking.

We were all shaken. His cataclysmic, overwhelming sadness shook me to the core. "Happiness was but the occasional episode in a general drama of pain," was how Thomas Hardy put it. I was just beginning to understand that the tennis, the beer, the comradeship and the laughs were my "occasional episodes of happiness". John's attempted suicide brought home to me that Psychiatric nursing seemed centred around the devastating emotional pain of other people's lives.

............................

Peggy and John loved each other so much. They so wanted to care for each other, but this was not always easy. After the suicide attempt John was finally allowed out on weekend leave with Peggy. He had been given strict instructions; if he had any problems he was not to worry but to come back immediately. At that point he was still on huge doses of anti-psychotic medication. One of the many side effects of these was increased salivation. John would talk as if blowing bubbles and, if he stood to talk to you, he'd have saliva dribbling down his chin which would be splattered all over you as well. He was put on a new medication, Artane, to stop the excess salivation. But the Artane itself had side effects. Peggy was given the Artane tablets to look after. I remember Ron pointing to the little bottle of tablets and telling her, "This is Artane. This is new. This is to help his salivation – to help his extra spit. O.K.?"

Peggy took the extra tablets, and we said goodbye. "See you tomorrow night."

Later that day I saw Peggy and John come through the door of the ward. I despaired. As they walked up the corridor towards the office I watched Peggy and John walking hand in hand. They had only been gone for about 8 hours. As they got closer I saw that John had a thick string of saliva hanging from his mouth, leaving a trail on the lino.

"Hi Peggy. You're back early. Problems?"

"He's dribbling everywhere. I can't have him home like this," she replied.

"Did you give him the Artane?"

"No. He didn't need it. He was dribbling so well, I decided not to give him any."

Good communication is vital. Peggy thought that the Artane was to MAKE him salivate, not to stop him. We had not communicated well.

Peggy and John were a semi-permanent fixture on Ward 24. Their extreme mood swings were an ongoing problem. Theirs was a terrible affliction, so disabling. Yet, despite the circumstances, I remain struck by their love for each other.

...............................

Alice was already in her bed when I arrived for an afternoon shift. 83 years old, she was waiting for the admitting doctor to "do the medical". This done she would be allowed up, usually in a dressing gown, until it was determined whether she was a risk to herself or others. A new patient in a dressing gown reduced the chances of escaping down the road. As usual for a new admission Alice was in the bed behind the window of the office.

She had been admitted for assessment under The Mental Health Act. "Sectioned Patients", those who were admitted formally, under a section, had their freedom restricted until an assessment of their mental state could be made.

The social worker sat in the office with Ron. She was at ease with him, chatting away as I walked in to join them. Ron had begun collecting the clinical information, usually a job for the nursing staff. I sat quietly, listening to the story of Alice's life.

"So Alice has a small rented terraced house. Does she live alone?"

"Never been married, as far as I know," said the social worker. "This is her first admission to any hospital in our area, as far as I can find out in the records."

"Does anyone look after her? Anyone cook her meals or the like?" asked Ron.

"No. But she's rarely at home until late evening. She's a working woman, always has been."

Ron continued to make notes. "What was her work?"

The social worker fiddled with her file. "She still works. I saw her working just last week," She continued. "I passed her in the car. She's been a prostitute all her adult life. She's told me all about it."

"Don't suppose she gets much trade now?" quipped Ron, seeking more information.

"No. She doesn't get many takers. ....just the odd one or two. Those that buy her services, pay her with a bit of food. Afterwards."

"Does she work from home or on the street?"

"No, never from home. She works out of a pub across town, "The Live and Let Live".

Here was another of those jolts to my preconceptions, perhaps a combination of my youth and my naivety. It would never have entered my head that a woman of this sort of age would still work in such a profession. As I approach my dotage I rarely receive such jolts now.

And where else would a working geriatric prostitute hang out?

The "Live and Let Live" Public House. I wondered what the beer was like!

# CHAPTER TWENTY-TWO

"Who the fuck are you?" It was 1.30 in the morning. I'd only done a few night shifts. I willed the staff nurse to appear. She didn't. I willed anyone at all to appear. They didn't. "Who the fuck are you?" I was on my own.

"I'm Stuart. I'm a student nurse," I said hurriedly, laying emphasis on the "student", trying to deflect aggression elsewhere, as quickly as possible. "If you just go back to your room, I'll get the staff nurse to come and talk to you." No response. I was facing a patient who, although still under the influence of substances unknown to me, recognised an open door when it stood right in front of him.

"Why the fuck would I want to see a stupid fucking nurse? Where the fuck are my clothes? Get me my fucking clothes, then I'm off." I was petrified. My eyes flicked again to the bottom of the corridor. Still no sign.

"I'm afraid that as you're sectioned......," I could already see the end my sentence and its consequences, "you're not allowed to leave yet." My lack of conviction was obvious.  "If you just go back ....." I tried to point to his room. But my arm failed to even reach the perpendicular.

My head banged against the wall. His hands gripped my throat. My head hurt. My mind was racing. I had no idea what to do. The news would report my death. Next of Kin would be informed......

..........Nights are for sleeping. My body tells me this. My body is not wrong.

179

Student nurses had to experience night duty. My first stint on nights was on Ward 24, my acute ward. I soon learnt that nights were not for me. The charge nurse on that first shift hated working days. "Nights are good, more money, less work and more days off." The life of a night nurse was like the life of a front line soldier, 99% boredom, and 1% frightening action. It was definitely not my thing. Apart from the medications, there was little to do on nights, no doctors rounds, no occupational therapy and no mealtimes. The patients usually drifted off to bed when TV finished, around 11 o'clock.

Yet a new admission made you suddenly aware just how vulnerable and isolated you were. With only two staff on the male side and two staff on the female side, with often just one male nurse in these four, a new admission could cause real problems.

Night admissions always had an edge. A night admission usually meant trouble. If the patient were controllable they would have waited till the morning, which was what the hospital doctor would have always preferred. It was the night nurse's job to insist that a doctor attended to "do the admission" and make sure that appropriate sedation was left for use after the doctor had gone. The last thing the night nurse wanted was the doctor disappearing back to "slumber land" only to discover that the patient had started destroying the ward and attacking the staff.

One of the few improvements in nurse training today is the training in the management of violence and aggression. In my days there was none. The older charge nurses just seemed to wade in, matching violence with violence. It was as though they were an offshoot of the Israeli army. They went in heavy handed and rarely had to go in twice.

There was no separate unit for patients with drug or alcohol problems, so those diagnosed with addiction problems involving violence, were taken to the acute units, usually under a section. More than 90% of patients at the asylum were termed "informal", and so they could, in theory, walk out - they couldn't be detained against their will. The other 10% were on some form of "section" under The Mental Health Act, which allowed for them to be detained, if necessary by force, until the section was removed by a psychiatrist.

Patients high on illicit drugs took some handling, being volatile, unpredictable and prone to violence. Violence, especially male violence, was so foreign, so frightening to me that I never got to grips with it. With the old stagers, I was more confident that we would be in control. For me the most frightening aspect of violence is the lack of any sense of where it will all end. With the older charge nurses around I always knew the result; they'd win.

...............................

On this particular night I had received details of a new patient who'd been admitted during the evening. Wayne, unhelpfully defined in handover as a "druggy", the disparaging term used, had come into the ward in a fighting mood, high on illegal drugs. An injection after tea had "settled him" and he was now sleeping. As he was a sectioned patient, he was not allowed to leave the ward. It was part of my duty to make sure he didn't. We didn't lock doors, so I was the metaphorical door preventing his escape.

There was just a female Staff Nurse and myself on duty that night and she had wandered down the corridor to pay a visit to the female end of the ward. I was alone, standing in the entrance of the male end, thinking about my Tupperware supper, which I'd eat once she returned.

I was distracted by a slight noise down the corridor where Wayne was supposed to be sleeping. A door slowly opened. I watched apprehensively as a figure slipped out of one of the rooms. It could only be Wayne. In pyjama bottoms and a dressing gown tied with a belt borrowed from the ward cache of communal clothes, he spotted me. Although the words were slurred, the menace was clear.

"Who the fuck are you?"

.............................

And now my head was throbbing and his hands were round my throat. There was nothing I could do. I was going to die.....

........They used to talk of the fight/flight mechanism in response to danger. Nowadays they talk of the fight/flight/freeze mechanism. I was an Olympic medalist in the freeze bit. Woody Allen and I would be competing for gold. I could hear my old tutor, Betty, warning me. I'd be found in the morning, dead under some smelly mattress.

There was a sudden shout as three female nurses came out of the dining room. Like a pride of enraged lionesses they charged up the corridor. Wayne stood and faced them, dropping his grip on my throat, bracing himself for a scrap. It took him less than two seconds to realise these females had made mincemeat of better and tougher men than him. His posture altered. He didn't do "freeze", just "flight". He made a dash for his room. But they were on him. At this stage I joined in. Why not? Holding an arm much more tightly than needed, I heroically helped as the lionesses bundled him to the floor.

One of them grabbed a needle, syringe and a vial of chlorpromazine from the clinic and, without the professional bedside manner, jammed 100mgs into his thigh muscle. He had more than met his match and was frog-marched unceremoniously back to his room and told in no uncertain terms what they'd do to him next time he attacked anyone. His muscular reputation had been smashed by this troop of women. However, my self-esteem had not exactly blossomed. I was just no good at all at handling physical violence.

........................

Some days later I was working with Kenny, Hughie's opposite number. Much of his time was spent studying the horses, gazing through the form. Unlike Hughie, everyone enjoyed working with Kenny. He was levelheaded and thoughtful. But it was with Kenny that I was to see how things had been done in the old days.

Wayne had spent some days out of the lime light, keeping to his room, after the fracas on his first night. But as his medication was reduced he started to spend more and more time in the centre of the ward where he could mix with the female patients. He was finding his feet, regaining his confidence and realising that many of the female patients were vulnerable and easily exploited. It would be so easy for Wayne to gratify his needs. Primarily he wanted money for more drugs, or alcohol, or both. However, he also he wanted his sexual desires fulfilled. The former wish was usually unfulfilled, as most patients had no immediate access to cash. His sexual desires came to the fore when a female patient not only refused him money, but also spurned his sexual demands. Hughie initially had a word with Wayne about his violence towards women. Wayne first blamed his violence towards women on his addiction, but then added the age-old lie "she was giving me the eye...." but nothing more was done.

Wayne believed he had a right to any female he wanted. A few days later another female patient was attacked. A female nurse, who went to help, was also hit, requiring a trip to the general hospital for stitches.

Kenny was on duty that day. Kenny wasn't Hughie. Kenny was to show me what they did in the old days.

"Stuart, draw up a hundred milligrams of chlorpromazine." I did as I was told, filled the syringe and took it through to Wayne's empty side room.

"Come on," said Kenny, "we need to deal with young Wayne."

Wayne was in the dining area of the Ward 24 and saw us as we entered.

Kenny was on him in the blink of an eye, grabbing him by both arms, lifting him from his chair and dragging him up the corridor. As he was dragged towards his room Kenny, professionalism set aside for the moment, calmly put the fear of God into Wayne.

"You'll fucking learn that attacking females isn't accepted here. You need to learn the consequences of your actions. You're going to get a little injection, you little prick!"

184

Wayne struggled, but Kenny was having none of it. He grabbed Wayne's head and locked it under his right arm. Kenny's left hand grabbed Wayne's hair and Wayne was dragged unceremoniously by his hair and head up the corridor to his room. Wayne's arms waved uselessly behind him as he was dragged along. I had nothing to hold or do, so I held open the door. Wayne was thrown into the room and pushed face down on his bed. Kenny leapt on top of him grinding his knee in the small of his back.

"You listen to me, you little shit. If you EVER, EVER attack a woman again I'll come looking for you." Kenny still had Wayne's hair in his left hand. He yanked hard on the hair stretching Wayne's neck to its limit. "Remember what I say, you little shit! You will NEVER, EVER do this again! Now you'll have your injection."

Still kneeling on top of him, Kenny ripped down Wayne's trousers, pointed at his thigh, not his buttock, and told me to give him the jab. A thigh injection is much more painful than a buttock injection. I unsheathed the needle, checked there were no air bubbles and looked to see that the muscle was readily available. As I was about to give the injection Kenny took the syringe off me, winked, then tapped the needle three times on the top of the steel trolley.

"Now, give him the jab."

I pressed the needle into Wayne's thigh, discharging the contents into his muscle. As I pulled the needle out Wayne screamed. The barb of the needle, created by Kenny's taps, would be a painful reminder for some time of the consequences of his nasty behaviour. He hobbled about for another week, only emerging from his room for meals. A week later he was discharged. He attacked no more women while he was on the ward. Whether Wayne had fully learned the consequences of his actions, I never knew. A violent, manipulative sociopath such as Wayne could wreak havoc on the lives of the vulnerable and depressed patients of a hospital like St. Paul's. For once Kenny had made a woman beater aware that there were unpleasant consequences for such behaviour.

Retribution did stalk the wards of St. Paul's, occasionally.

..........................

Just a few shifts after this melee, I was at work when an auxiliary nurse wandered onto the ward. Three staff on the male side was not known, two was the usual maximum, so I expected some other staff change to occur.

"The nursing officer has asked that you do tonight's shift at the acute clinic attached to the general hospital. I'm here to fill in for you."

The acute clinic was a stand-alone unit attached to the general hospital. By the late 70s it was felt that acute psychiatry needed to be seen as just another a branch of medicine, to gradually bring it within the fold of general medicine. Hence these new acute units. They were built to a set plan, with mirror images around the country. They all looked like large prefabricated cabins. Despite their lack of style or substance, working in the general hospital setting was probably the highest kudos of psychiatric nursing. Of course, the old stagers decried it as a sop to general nursing's supposed superiority.

I arrived as handover was finishing. I knew nobody on the unit. I looked around. It was all very different. It was modern. It was high tech. It was dynamic. It was horrible.

Half a dozen police had brought in a man in his thirties. The man, in handcuffs, had been sectioned in order to assess his mental state. He had been admitted, against his will, for assessment following a particularly nasty axe attack in the city, in which the victim had lost part of his arm. Due to the problems the police had had in arresting him, it had been decided that, following an injection of chlorpromazine, he needed to be retained in this safe environment, to determine if he was "mentally ill".

There were five night staff normally on the clinic at night, but as one was off sick, I had been told to "lend my weight". What became obvious, from watching the end of the handover, was that all the male staff were going off duty. I had been brought in as the token male. The box could now be ticked that a male staff member was on the rota for that night. If trouble kicked off the authorities could say that they had ensured safety. I was that safety. Little, at that stage, did any of the regulars know of my uselessness. Clint Eastwood I wasn't. I wouldn't be threatening anyone with "make my night."

The charge nurse, Terry, came to see me. "He's had his injection, so will probably be quiet for the night. If he wakes and starts to cause trouble, make sure you've got other staff members with you. He's quite a handful." I particularly noted the adjective "probably" when Terry was prophesying the axman's future somnolence. I would have rather had a more definite adverb. "Certainly" would have been more welcome.

With those parting words Terry was off for a good night's sleep, leaving me as the heavy. All I could hope was that the females would be as clannish and protective as the ones on Ward 24.

That night was long and fearful for me. I was put on a chair outside his room, with vague instructions to give everyone a shout if he got out. I didn't need reminding of that instruction. As the night progressed I surreptitiously moved the chair to opposite the door, reasoning that this allowed me to watch the door and not have my back to it. In reality it was, for me, a clever ploy. Across the corridor I could be just anybody, not a nurse, not a staff member, not necessarily "guarding" the axe man. Following this theme, within the first hour I had removed my white coat and tie. Now slumped in a chair with open-necked shirt, no coat and therefore no name badge, I could be anyone, just another patient perhaps, having a quiet nap. It was a considered adjustment to the original placing of me next to his room. It might save me from having an axe buried in my head. It was a good ploy.

We were not allowed to lock the doors to patients' rooms, a retrograde step I decided that night, so we would have to rely on either psychiatric skills to talk him down (I had none) or brute force (the same). As the night wore on I watched where other staff were settling. Were they in easy shouting distance? Would they rush to my rescue if the axe wielder made an escape bid? Lastly, had anyone actually mentioned what had happened to the axe?

Without having seen the man, indeed, I didn't even know his name, my mind pictured him as huge, strong, muscles like Popeye, staring eyes and the rationality of a rabid dog. Each sound coming from the room made me jump. What use could I be? Why hadn't they left him handcuffed? Each hour seemed to be two and I watched the time pass, willing the day shift to come in early and let me go. It was the longest night of all my night shifts. Given how much I hated nights, this was really saying something.

The clock ticked down to seven a.m. Fifteen minutes to go, ten minutes to go, five minutes to go..... At long last Terry arrived, promptly, at seven in the morning. "Is he ok?" he asked. I didn't tell him that as far as I was concerned the man could have died hours ago. I had not clapped eyes on him. I certainly wouldn't think of going in to wake him up through the night, to make sure of his welfare. "Let sleeping dogs lie" was Prime Minister Robert Walpole's adage in the early 1700s. Who was I to argue? As far as I was concerned he was either asleep or dead. I really didn't care which as long as he maintained this inert state in his room with the door closed.

But without so much as a blink of an eye, and definitely not waiting for a considered response from me, Terry strode into the man's room, shook him awake and told him to get up for breakfast time. The commanding way he did this suggested that, to Terry, patients like this were small potatoes in the great scheme of things. Terry came out, thanked me for my help during the night, and told me that I would be there again tonight. I made my way home, ruminating as I went, considering another night like the last.

I slid into bed, mentally exhausted, but not before phoning my tutor to tell her that I was suffering from a heavy cold and would not be in that night. After one day's sick, followed by two days off, the acute clinic had settled down. I was no longer needed, or perhaps they just weren't that desperate. I never asked what was the outcome of the mad axe man. I was just so pleased that my next shift was back on Ward 24.

# CHAPTER TWENTY-THREE

Hughie would often wax lyrical about his knowledge, always with a beaming toothy smile, but I used Ron for gaining knowledge of acute psychiatry, trying, where possible, to work shifts with him. Ron had a sense of humour that I understood, whereas I never grasped Hughie's.

In a handover, it transpired that an older patient named Leonard, who had a long history of schizophrenia and came in regularly to get his medication stabilised, had complained of constipation. Despite various medicines to "unblock" him, these treatments had failed. His abdomen had become distended.

Hughie, perhaps aware that he hadn't actually trained me in anything announced, at the end of handover, that he would show me how to give an enema. On Ward 7 I had administered a number of enemas. Being a geriatric ward, it was where enemata would be taught. But Hughie wanted to show me how to "do it properly", Jack's teaching obviously insufficient. Ron grinned at the thought. "You'll probably enjoy this. Getting a lesson from Hughie is definitely a lesson you'll never forget. I guarantee you'll never use it again."

"Now then boy," said Hughie with a grin even wider than usual, "let me show you the equipment you need." He never bothered to enquire if this procedure was something I needed to learn. It was a practical procedure, so Hughie possibly thought that not much could go wrong. He wanted to show me that he could teach students with the best.

With that he was off to the sluice room, where he climbed on a chair to reach a high shelf. From here he retrieved a tin jug, a funnel and a length of orange rubber tubing, cracked and stiff. He opened the drug cupboard and took out a brown medicine bottle with the words "Liquid Soap" on the peeling and stained label. The bottle had probably been placed there between the wars.

In the School of Nursing we had been taught the theory about enemas. But this particular equipment was only mentioned as a relic of the old days, a museum piece to wonder at. Yet here we were reclaiming it from the past. "Hughie, I thought that all this tubing and things had been replaced now with disposable enemas. Surely we can't still be using these?" It was a futile question. Hughie never changed direction on anything. He was unable to face being told by anyone, let alone a student nurse, of changes that had passed him by.

"This is the way I was taught, boy, and this is the way I do it. Learn from me and you'll not go far wrong." The voice always had the same tone, rather like patronising plainchant.

A large dash of liquid soap was diluted with warm water in the jug. A tube of lubricating jelly was put on the trolley, along with a gauze swab, and away we went to the dormitory. Leonard had been placed on his own bed at the far end, lying down, on his left side, with his pyjamas on, under a blanket. Ron had placed him there and then escaped quickly. He was looking forward to the outcome, but certainly didn't want to get involved, or to be seen to watch the inevitable disaster. Hughie pronounced, "just watch me, boy, then you'll see how to do this." Using the gauze swab he wiped the jelly around the end of the tube, pulled down Leonard's pyjama trousers and inserted the nozzle into his rectum. He held the nozzle in place, turning to me to direct my part of the proceedings.

"Now, hold up the funnel, boy, and slowly pour in the liquid."

"How much should pour in?"

"The phrase to remember, boy, when giving an enema, is the three 'H's', high, hot, a hell of a lot. So pour it all in, boy. No point in wasting any."

So I slowly poured. The pint or more of warm liquid slowly glugged its way through the tube coming to rest in Brian's rectum. When it was all gone I put down the jug.

"What happens now, Hughie?"

"We wait, boy. We just wait," he intoned.

We duly waited, in silence. After about five minutes Leonard started to wriggle. Until now he had been the forgotten patient, as I had been watching Hughie and Hughie had been watching the anus to ensure the tube stayed in.

"Want to go to toilet Sir," muttered Leonard, as he started to move, shuffling to the edge of the bed.

Hughie looked at me. His face was suddenly alert. The grin had gone. He realised that there had been an error. Worse than this, he realised HE had made an error. But much worse, he knew that I knew he'd made an error.

The ooze was starting to seep out. There were no commodes in the acute unit. The toilets were at the other end of the dormitory, a long way for a leaky rectum. There was no solution. I could see Hughie trying desperately to think of a solution, to save face. But time was something that Leonard, hadn't got.

"Take him up to the toilets, boy. I think he may be a bit desperate," was Hughie's understated instruction.

I wanted to say "You take him, then we'll all see what a pig's ear you've made of this," but didn't. I rolled Leonard into an upright position, pulling his pyjamas up as I moved him and took him by the hand through the dormitory, holding the back of his pyjama bottoms with my other hand to stop them from falling. The pyjamas quickly filled. Should we walk quickly or slowly? Which would cause less leakage? How could Leonard walk quickly whilst trying to retain such a quantity of fluid? Never mind that his buttocks were clenched, his knees were locked as well for extra support.

As Leonard hobbled the trickle of sludge became a stream and then a full torrent as his rectum could no longer cling on. Farting and spraying through the pyjamas he increased his speed, breaking into a run. Clinging to the pyjama bottoms, I was dragged along with him. We raced down the ward. It was as uncoordinated as a three-legged race. As we ran his feet kicked up the excrement, leaving a nasty trail in our wake. We reached the toilet for him to sit down with a sigh. I removed his, by now brown, pyjamas and covered him in a dressing gown. Leonard was no longer constipated. I ran the bath. Leonard would need a long, a very long, soak.

I returned to the dormitory. The floor and many of the counterpanes were covered. All the beds would require stripping and remaking. The trolley was still there, with the tubing left dangling over the edge of the lower shelf. I would need to find a mop and bucket to start to clear up the mess on the floor. The stench was terrible. Of Hughie, there was no sign. Nothing was said, although a quick note was made in the day report that an enema had been performed. Ron dined out on the story for weeks.

Changes can be for the better or the worse. The switch from tubing and liquid soap enemas to disposable enemas was a distinct improvement. If I were to do an enema again I would keep to the modern method.

I'd also make sure there was a receptacle nearby for the patient.

Hughie's only teaching session was consigned to the same bin as the funnel and tubing.

# CHAPTER TWENTY-FOUR

No one ever forgot Marie. Despite the pretty name, she was a sad fixture for most staff at some time or another.

Marie had been on the female end of Ward 24 for nearly six months, but her admission, on a formal section, followed only a couple of weeks after a previous stay of a year. On this section she could be treated against her will, and she was.

Although there were patients whose diagnoses were questionable, Marie was definitely not one of them. She had schizophrenia. Nowadays people are taught to separate the illness from the person, an admirable and correct approach. The primary objective in working with a patient is to attempt to understand them as a person, the illness being an awful add-on. It is all too easy for the illness to be an excuse to avoid the person behind the affliction. But with Marie the illness pervaded every aspect, causing her unending psychological pain and torture from the voices that plagued her and the visions that assaulted her.

Marie came from a broken background. She'd been brought up by a number of foster parents and had no known relatives. There seemed to be no one who had ever known her as a well person. Indeed, the only people to have known her for any length of time were the staff of the asylum, but they all knew her through her severe illness. No one visited her. The staff had become her next-of-kin.

She was huge, Eighteen stone at least. She had a round podgy face, with black eyes, often almost closed from the effects of sedation. Black greasy hair was uncombed and un-styled. She had never been a "looker". Most of the time I knew her she was dressed in the same outfit.: baggy pyjamas with buttons missing, a toweling dressing gown, with SP on the back but no toweling belt, for fear of self-strangulation. These were her usual day clothes. The dressing gown was almost always open, her very ample cleavage regularly bursting forth on the unsuspecting. On the rare occasions when she did wear normal clothes, they were ill fitting, ward supplied, cotton tracksuits. If Marie wore slippers they were usually odd ones and often only one, which usually fell off. Generally she wandered in her blackened bare feet.

Marie smiled, not as a reaction to humour but when the voices told her to smile. Her conversations were all with the voices. Her concentration, what little she had, could only focus on the voices. Nothing else seemed to be heard. She took little notice of speech directed to her by us, our speech drowned out by the volume of her own auditory hallucinations. Marie was a tragic person with no discernible happiness in her life.

At twenty-eight she looked forty-eight. She was unable to make friends on the ward, instead spending her time wandering around talking to the voices, or perhaps screaming at them. There was no peace for Marie and never would be. As the torments had continued and increased so she had increased in her self-harm, whether by ligature, knife or scalding water. She required constant supervision to keep her alive. Her most recent admission had been as the result of throwing herself into a canal in an attempt to drown herself. But she could, and did, swim. Failure at that attempt made her even angrier as the voices tormented her regarding this abject failure, laughing at her ongoing inabilities.

About two-thirds of people with schizophrenia do quite well on the anti-psychotic medications. About 10% of those with schizophrenia seem to gain nothing from the medications, apart from side effects. Marie was at the extreme end of this group. Her psychiatrist Dr Candle had treated her since she was a teenager, but with no real success. Psychiatrists want success. They need success. Without it they feel impotent. Without success they fall back on their only option - increase the medications. Surely, they felt, at some point the anti-psychotic effect would start to work. Just a little more.......

Not for Marie. At each ward round when her name came up Dr Candle would ask how she was progressing. He would be told of the shouting, screaming, maniacal presentation. She would be brought into the ward round, accompanied by two members of staff, to confirm this untreatable deteriorating presentation.

Marie was very aggressive with just about everyone. The aggression was determined by what the voices told her to do, with the result that her attacks came out of the blue. The voices would instruct her to launch an attack on a patient or member of staff. She was powerless to resist. However, these attacks were always isolated incidents. Marie bore no grudges against anyone, but couldn't resist the overwhelming force of her voices. There was one exception, Dr Candle. It felt to me that, when the voices told her to kill Dr Candle, this was the one instruction that she didn't even try to resist. Dr Candle was Marie's sworn enemy.

I was never in fear of Marie. I would sit with her when possible or walk with her when she was agitated. I grew to know when she was a potential or actual danger. Her eyes would stare at a person, talking quietly to herself, or rather her voices, about what she'd do to them. Then she would stand and slowly move towards them. Marie didn't usually move fast but it needed a quick decision from me whether to turn her around, or move the person who I knew was in the firing line. Mostly she would allow this to happen, but sometimes she'd break away, launching her attack anyway. Either way she seemed to accept that I was doing my job. In a funny way, I loved being with her.

The only time that she moved fast was when Dr Candle was in sight. She was determined to cause him pain. As her threat escalated he would phone the ward to warn if he was attending, allowing us to get Marie out of sight. I was present one day when Dr Candle arrived to check in a new patient. He had been elsewhere in the asylum and decided that he could "do the medical" before leaving for his private work. This was a mistake. He had failed to ring the nurses first. He appeared through the large doors, which swung closed behind him. Marie was next to me at the other end of the day room. The slight noise of the doors closing triggered her to lift her heavy eyes towards the noise. The trap was sprung. She was out of the chair in an instant, moving with a speed I hadn't seen before. A table in the middle of the room was spun over spilling books and cups onto the floor. Dr Candle noticed the charging patient and backed into a corner, but in that split second Marie was on him, punching, kicking and gouging. I was on her as well, gripping her arm, hooking a leg over her thrashing legs. Slobber sprayed the fight.

It was over in a minute with staff rushing to contain Marie. Dr Candle got out with scrapes and scratches. I thought Marie looked happier following the attack. Dr Candle decided to increase the medication again.

By the time I left the acute ward Marie was on medication levels that were not just high, but off the scale. Chlorpromazine usually had a range of 25mgs-100mgs up to three times a day. Marie was on 500mgs four times a day. Haloperidol usually has a range of 0.5mgs to 5mgs. Marie was on 40mgs four times a day. On top of that she was on a huge dose of depot injection and, following a further attack, was on 20mls of Paraldehyde four times a day. All these medications were taken together, in a large glass beaker. As she drank it her level of sedation would lead to her being unable to hold the liquid in her mouth and the orange coloured fluid would run down her fleshy jowls onto her already stained dressing gown. The Paraldehyde gave her, and the ward, that stench.

She was no better for this, but maintained her delusions and hallucinations on top of the massive side effects of the medication. Ron would say that she'd probably be better off without any medication. In time I came to think he might be right.

Marie died a few years later. She never left the acute unit again. Although psychiatry can be very sad, with despair and trauma in so many patients, Marie was possibly the saddest I ever met. There never seemed to be any remission, nor any form of happiness in any part of her troubled and relatively short existence. I look at past patients finding transition between the good and the bad times. Poor Marie appeared to have no transition. It was just bad times. To see her, so drugged up she could hardly stand, with saliva running down her chin, responding to voices that created such fear, yet without any relief, was a demoralising snapshot for a young student nurse. Marie. Untreatable.

But I also remember the kindness shown to her by the ward staff. They all recognised her terrible plight. When some modern writers denied schizophrenia as an illness, and in those days various authors were doing just that, the memory of her brings back the reality of the true horror of this terrible disease.

# CHAPTER TWENTY-FIVE

When Electro Convulsive Therapy, E.C.T., began to be used widely, it was a treatment primarily in the acute units. This was especially due to its relative simplicity of procedure. A box, named the Ectonus Machine, was the only equipment required, so from the late 1940s E.C.T. was used for just about every ailment in the psychiatric lexicon.

One of the problems of E.C.T. was fracture and dislocation of the long bones of patients, as the patients, although held down by staff, thrashed about from the induced seizure. Straight E.C.T., that is E.C.T. without any form of anaesthesia, was a clumsy tool, so short-acting muscle-relaxant medications were given to reduce the problem. However, the feeling of paralysis brought on by the muscle relaxant, the inability to breathe, caused panic in patients. They felt they were slowly suffocating. To deal with this it was decided to anaesthetise them as well. However, this made the procedure more complicated, with the need for an anaesthetist and a doctor to administer the shock. This more humane method was termed "modified E.C.T." From the late 1960s modified E.C.T. was the accepted method of treatment.

Modified E.C.T. was one of the ward routines every Tuesday and Friday. The ward doctor, either the consultant psychiatrist or the registrar, would do the "zapping" as staff called it; holding the electrodes to the skull and pressing the button of the show-boxed size "Ectonus" machine. It was a boring repetitive procedure which involved a cluster of doctors and nurses standing round waiting - waiting for staff to arrive, waiting for patients to arrive, waiting for patients to wake up, waiting for patients to go.

While Jack was working on Ward 24 in the early 1970s one particular female anaesthetist would insist on starting at the female side of Ward 24. She had the habit of stopping for a coffee after the female session before wandering over to deal with the males. Jack remembered the male psychiatrist becoming increasingly agitated at having to wait around for the anaesthetist, something that he had done too many times before. Complaining to Jack that his time was too precious to waste, the psychiatrist ordered Jack to get the three patients lying down ready. All three were then given straight E.C.T., without anaesthesia or muscle relaxant. Staff were fully involved trying to contain and protect patients from broken or dislocated limbs, and also trying to reassure waiting patients who could see their fellows thrashing wildly about and having to be restrained while they were being "zapped". Panic all around, but no one challenged the psychiatrist. It just wasn't done.

I was present when a young woman, Sarah, was admitted to the female end of Ward 24. She was twenty-three years old, married to Graham, and came in accompanied by Graham and their four-week-old daughter. Sarah had a diagnosis of post-natal depression. I was the one to show Sarah her bed. Initially she would be in a side room so that she could have time with her daughter, but if she was seen as a risk, she would be moved to the bed by the window of the office, the mirror position to John's on the male side.

Taking her and her husband through to her new room was a quiet affair. No one spoke until I pushed open the heavy door. Pale blue walls, cold, a wood-framed bed, tatty, and a chest of drawers, broken, were all that greeted her. Over the next few days her husband, Graham, brought in some items to make it feel slightly more homely. The homely objects never took disguised the reality that this was an asylum side room, used in the past as a locked cell.

Sarah never spoke during those first two months. Her eyes never focused. She had to be fed, having no apparent volition of her own. Graham came to see her most days, sometimes with their baby daughter, but she showed no apparent reaction. She had been on anti-depressant medication since before she was admitted, but her mood never lifted, her blackness remained. Graham's devotion and love never palled as he sat and talked to her, without any obvious reaction from Sarah. The medication had no effect, leading to the psychiatrists increasing the doses, and then changing to other types of anti-depressants. This was the usual route taken with patients with persistent and what seemed to be untreatable psychiatric illness. There was only one stage left. E.C.T.

Sarah was beyond refusing E.C.T. and Graham, by now, would try anything. She had been mute and generally unresponsive for months. Her daughter was growing up without a mother. Graham was providing, along with his parents, the security and love a daughter needed, but she also needed her real mother.

I was on duty that Tuesday when she had her first E.C.T. Having been involved with the E.C.T. on the male end of the ward, once I had finished the checks on our male patients, I walked over to the female end to see how Sarah was, following her "shock". Graham was with her. The staff nurse grinned and suggested I say hello to her. The Sarah I met was not the same as the one I knew. This one was chatty, gregarious and "normal". She talked to Graham, with me butting in occasionally, of what she felt, how she'd missed her daughter, and how soon she could go home to be with her. Her eyes were bright; she was animated and responsive. Overall she was just charming. It was a miracle. I left her to be with Graham. I felt almost as elated as Graham. At last, acute psychiatry had done something special.

By the Wednesday Graham's parents had arrived. She was allowed to go out for the day to be with her daughter. I saw her again on the Thursday before her next E.C.T. The staff were still elated at her improvement, although they felt she had slipped slightly in her emotions since that Tuesday. More E.C.T. was carried out. Sarah had weekend leave, returning on the Tuesday for her next treatment. However, she was now quieter and more subdued. Was this due to worries over the procedure, I wondered? After the third E.C.T., the lights somehow seemed to be shutting down again. She was no longer as interested in talking, listening, sharing. After ten treatments she was mute again. The treatment was stopped. The anti-depressants were increased. Three months later, with Sarah still mute, E.C.T. was restarted, all to no avail. Her return to sanity was only brief. Further E.C.T.s made no effect. The daughter would never get the mother she needed.

Psychologists were sent for who assessed her over long periods but found no solutions. By the time I last saw her staff could be forgiven for quietly muttering that the mutism and depression might have had something to do with Sarah's relationship with Graham. "Perhaps she doesn't want to get better. Perhaps it's due to problems in her childhood" (always a safe fall back). We knew that Sarah was not returning to normality, so it was easier to think of it as perhaps Sarah's fault, or Graham's fault, rather than our own professional impotence.

E.C.T. could have remarkable short-term results, but in the longer term it seemed to have little going for it. The positive impact faded quickly after the initial jolt. The psychiatrists, in the same way that they increased medication, increased the number of E.C.T.s a patient had to bear, leading to some having hundreds. As the E.C.T.s increased, in number and power, there was no discernible improvement. The psychiatrists would say that if the first E.C.T. led to a 40% improvement, then further treatments would produce even better results. But in my experience they never did.

It has been argued that as we don't know how E.C.T. works we shouldn't give it. However, we are still uncertain as to how most psychiatric medications work, but still prescribe and administer them. Is this OK? The arguments about E.C.T. have raged since I was a student nurse and continue today.  Studies into its usefulness have been, to say the least, inconclusive. One survey showed that patients being anaesthetised in expectation of E.C.T., and then NOT having the shock, had the same degree of improvement as those anaesthetised and "zapped".  But other studies are contradictory. No one can agree on the benefits of E.C.T. or its harm.

It is with some shame that I remember a student nurse in the year behind me at St. Paul's, whom I shall call Ben. I hardly knew him, but soon heard of his reputation. Due to the arguments raging about the efficacy of E.C.T., whether it was treatment or an abuse, Ben researched the treatment and decided that, as it was not a proven to work and, as it caused some degree of brain damage, he would refuse to take part in any further treatments. This was a brave stand, which soon got the local, and then national, newspapers involved. He was threatened with dismissal.

A local MP and the Minister of State for Health became involved. I'm sure it was an unwelcome addition to their parliamentary work. The asylum responded by insisting that as E.C.T. was a treatment that was offered at St. Paul's, Ben must take part. He bravely refused. Other staff then muttered that if he was allowed to avoid this treatment, they might have the right to opt out of any treatments they didn't like. Charge nurses felt that if Ben was going to refuse to participate, they didn't want him on their ward.

I, to my shame, sided with the asylum and the charge nurses. Ben eventually moved to another hospital where they didn't use E.C.T. and received his R.M.N. qualification from there. E.C.T. did become a treatment that was optional for student nurses to attend and participate in. As I look back I am full of admiration for Ben and for the moral stance he took. What happened to him I don't know, but I hope he made a success of his career. He was a principled man.

E.C.T. continues to be given occasionally as a treatment for severe depressions. There remain people, people I respect, who consider it a vital option in severe and psychotic depressions. Yet even these admit that its usefulness is generally short term. I feel that jolting the brain with such a burst of electricity is not something I would recommend, but perhaps, if there seemed to be no options left, even a straw might be clutched. But, except as a last resort, I would fight tooth and nail to stop it being administered to anyone in my family.

.................................

The acute setting was my first experience of groups of people from differing professions chewing over the private minutiae of people's lives. Each group approached the problems from a baseline drilled into them by their own training. Whereas in long-stay and geriatrics the nurses, with occasional psychiatrist involvement, provided care that was on going, in acute wards other disciplines, in the late 1970s, were battling to build their own empires. "Interesting" patients were fought over. They could be used in "papers" delivered to professional bodies. There were few "interesting" patients in Ward 24, so the occasional fascinating one became a trophy to be fought for.

Nurses were the largest tribe within the asylum, but not the most powerful. This accolade belonged to the psychiatrists. In the general hospitals there was a saying: "physicians are just failed surgeons", so say the surgeons. From medical school, so the old wives' tale suggested, the brightest medical students went on to become surgeons; the less bright went on to become physicians and the more gregarious became GPs. Those who fitted into none of these categories became psychiatrists.

Psychiatrists gained the kudos of the position of "consultant" but were generally never treated with the respect they yearned for from their consultant colleagues in the general hospitals. Psychiatrists tended to be solitary creatures, often lacking the skills needed to lead a team. Yet, of the asylum groups, the nurses would usually side with the psychiatrists rather than any other. Nurses were the group that the psychiatrists could dictate to. The other professions "did their own thing". The nurses and psychiatrists had grown used to each other's peculiar ways. Through history both tribes "knew where the bodies were buried", whereas others didn't.

The Mental Health Act of 1959 did put some of the brakes on the excesses of the psychiatrists, but it took many years for this to become reality. Even in the late 70s the Mental Health Review Tribunal (MHRT), the "independent jury", which assessed whether a sectioned patient was a danger to themselves or others would be denigrated by psychiatrists. "Who are these people to question me?" they would ask.

During my first acute experience a psychiatrist was concerned that one of his patients had applied to be seen by the MHRT and to get himself discharged. The MHRT, a small group that included a doctor, lawyer and layperson, had the power to over-rule a Section. The psychiatrist ordered that the patient should be given a large dose of the drug Cogentin, on a one off basis, thereby causing agitation and psychosis. The patient was seen by the MHRT and his mental state was judged as so psychotic that the Section was confirmed. Release was impossible. The Cogentin had done the trick. The psychiatrist wanted him to remain in hospital. He wouldn't accept any interference from the MHRT

Despite the abusive incidents I saw from psychiatrists, along with their disproportionate power, the most striking aspect of psychiatrists was when, rarely, a good one turned up. A good psychologist could be a benefit. A good psychiatrist was a real game changer. In all my years in psychiatry I came across just four. But what a difference they made.

Psychologists were a rare breed in my time as a student nurse. I rarely saw them in the asylum. Psychologists don't come from a medical background. Their area of "expertise" is that of behaviour – not necessarily illness based at all, although, obviously, in a mental hospital, this was what they were supposed to be there for! I was usually told that they worked in the community setting, though I failed to spot them there either. Psychologists and psychiatrists were two very small but very powerful tribes driven by mutual suspicion and dislike. Some of this was rooted in money. Psychiatrists earned around fifty per cent more than psychologists, often for the same length of training. However the enmity was also based on a difference of beliefs. In the seventies psychiatrists usually believed that the cause of mental illness was based on some form of faulty wiring of the brain, whereas psychologists put the root cause as some form of faulty learning leading to poor relationships and problems in behaviour. It was the old "nature/nurture" divide. Psychologists were rarely given the responsibility for a patient that a psychiatrist had. But then psychologists didn't have beds. Beds were power. A patient could only be on a ward if under a psychiatrist. In the 70s a psychiatrist would need to be dragged kicking and screaming into referring a patient to a psychologist, and vice versa.

The last tribe, and the one that elicited most scorn from the other three, were the occupational therapists. Coming late to psychiatry, they never fitted easily into the three warring groups. Belittled by nurses as basket weavers and knitting gurus, they were also derided by the psychiatrists and psychologists as having little to offer either theoretically or practically. I remember an occupational therapist telling me that, in a general ward for stroke victims, the physiotherapist's job was to get patients to move and function, but it was the occupational therapist's job to get the patient to make a cup of tea, and walk with it to their chair. Yet occupational therapists struggled to see how they fitted into the factions of an asylum. As time progressed, occupational therapists tended to drop their own title, giving themselves grander epithets such as "behavioural therapists", "art therapists", "cognitive therapists", "play therapists" and "drama therapists". Most were only to glad to lose the title "occupational", a title that gave them a lower kudos than a porter. A "therapist" didn't have to admit their base training!

In time social workers would join this intemperate and warring system leading to the psychologists and the occupational therapists joining forces, and job titles, "the therapists", to try to balance the coalition of the psychiatrists and the nurses. The social workers generally remained outsiders, linking to their professional colleagues back at the welfare establishments rather than the professionals at the asylum.

Interesting patients were fought over by the tribes, for inclusion in obscure academic research, whilst the long stay and routine were passed to whoever could be corralled into accepting them, always the nurses and the psychiatrists.

Yet the nurses, therapists and particularly the psychiatrists although supposed experts in human behaviour and interactions, regularly seemed to have major problems with their own behaviour and interactions. All too often they had a background of failed relationships and failed friendships, leading to solitary existences without interests or close friends. Quite why someone would consult a professional with such obvious relationship flaws when it came to their own life was beyond me. One wouldn't take one's car to a garage where the mechanic was unable to keep his own car on the road.

The mutual distrust between the professionals of psychiatry continues to this day.

# CHAPTER TWENTY-SIX

I'm sad enough to love golf but the quality of my game doesn't bring me into contact with the "movers and shakers" of society. Indeed, I'm lucky just to get some mug to have their game ruined on the meaningless wander round the course.

Manic depression was the term used in the late 1970s for what is now termed bipolar disorder. Both terms refer to the second of the severe mental illnesses. There always seems to be a separation between schizophrenia and bipolar disorder in that schizophrenia is unrelenting whereas bipolar disorder is sporadic. Because of this, the sweep into the extremes of mood, whether depression or mania, appears all the more explosive. The unexpected nature of its unpredictability is always a surprise to family, friends and professionals. I would guess that bipolar disorder is the source of most of the stories from psychiatry. Devastating as the illness can be, when professionals talk of their experiences of bipolar disorder, it usually brings a smile.

The depression side of bipolar disorder presents like other depressions: low mood, lacking energy, feelings of low self-worth. It is the manic episodes that are odd. I think that there is an almost enviable quality to the manic episodes. For a period of time the self-belief, totally misguided, is so complete that the patient perceives that they have supreme ability, a sense that others never get, except possibly psychiatrists!

It was quite soon after starting on Ward 24 that Desmond, in his mid thirties, was admitted. He came in with a long history of bipolar disorder, always presenting to us in the manic phase. He wasn't sleeping, his speech was rushed and garbled but he had this total conviction that he was on the verge of becoming great. I met up with him when he had had a good night's sleep, due to medication. Yet he woke with the verve of fantastic enthusiasm. I asked him why he had come in.

"My wife, Pam, went to the doctor to get me admitted. It was only because I'd gone for a game of golf."

Talking to people in mania often leaves the questioner desperately trying to work out the meaning of the response. It's sometimes called "dogleg thinking". This dogleg thinking occurs with a speech rate that would probably enable of person with mania to cram the entire Bible onto one CD of a talking book! Keeping up with the discourse requires much concentration.

"Why, exactly, did a game of golf get you admitted?" I asked.

"I went up to the Royal Anglian Golf Club for a game of golf. Pam had to come over to pick me up. The next thing I knew I was admitted. How is it possible to get admitted for a game of golf? Jack Nicklaus doesn't get admitted does he?" Desmond pleaded.

"Are you a member there?"

"No, but it's the best club in the city. Always thought that. Others aren't as good. Great fairways, so I've heard."

I was trying to follow the logic. "So where do you usually play?"

"Nowhere," he answered. "But I'm starting up this company. It's going to make lots of money - millions. I read in the papers that most major business deals are done on the golf course. Well, I'm not a member of a golf club, but I knew that if this company was to work, I had to join. All the biggest deals are made there. I went to the Royal Golf Club to join. All the top people in the city play there. They'll all be there. Definitely. And...."

"So," I butted in "I presume you played golf in the past. Is that why you want to take it up again?"

"Never played in my life, but the golf club is where it's all happening. To get ahead you have to play golf. I'll learn. I can be a brilliant golfer. A few lessons and a few weeks practice. I'm a natural sportsman. I'll be bloody good."

"What will your business do?"

"Haven't decided yet, but it'll make money and lots of it. I bet Robert Maxwell plays golf. He'd sort out the deals there. Talking of Robert Maxwell, I need to sort out about a share issue. Get one of these original shares and you're made. I could start a newspaper empire. I could fly around going to ......" He stopped momentarily, trying to think of a place to fly to. One second later he switched. "Course, there are other sports, Polo, might need to buy a horse, but then maybe there aren't any pitches to play on. Do they call them pitches?" And so it went on.....

Hearing someone speak when they are in hyper mania is like listening to the rapid reading of six different books with all the punctuation marks removed.

...........................

We should have picked up the escalation of his grandiosity. The following day he went off the ward and returned at lunchtime. He'd been into town. He sprinted down to the dining room for lunch just as Sister White from the female side arrived to see Hughie. I was in the office writing up the patient notes.

"Hughie. Are there any visitors in on your side?"

"No, why?" asked Hughie.

"So whose Rolls-Royce is it in the car park?"

"What? God, let's go and see." With that they both raced off to the car park, with me in tow. There in the middle of the car park, parked across the marked lines, was a dark green Rolls Royce. It must have been about ten years old but this was no wreck. This was a quality machine.

Both stood silently, gazing at the Roller. "Well," said Hughie, "I think we now know how Desmond has spent his morning." Hughie paused and thought. "I'll have a word with him."

We found out that Desmond had been to town, stopped at the local Rolls-Royce dealers, convinced them of his financial worth and, with a down payment of £200, had driven off in a £8000 Roller. He needed it for his business. What else could he lift his golf clubs from? It took time to get the machine returned. The salesman at the car dealership took considerable persuasion to accept that the dealership would be best just to accept it back. They would have had a very considerable wait if the car were to be paid for by Desmond's new company, as promised. You can't learn golf in a day for a start.

It highlighted to me the believability of someone in mania. It is not that they want to be important, it is that they have total faith that they are important, thereby convincing others of their prowess.

215

But the real impact was on the relatives. At around the time I trained new rules were set in place, especially in the banking systems, that could protect families from the excesses of their manic relatives. Too often manic sufferers would trade in their own pension to put it all on the turn of the wheel in roulette, or sell the family house to plug a loophole in their grand schemes. For staff, dealing with the person could be amusing alternative to the humdrum routines. But to the wife or husband it must have been be a never-ending fear that pecuniary security could be blown on a horse with a cute face.

Mania has an addictive quality. Such complete belief and conviction is usually not a sense that a well person would ever get. People with bipolar disorder can feel at their most contented when they have these feelings; they rarely realise that the feelings are just that - feelings. The influence and status are illusionary. But compared to the low of depression the high is much preferable. Many with bipolar disorder take a drug, lithium carbonate, which keeps their mood "normal", but which they often say keeps them from feeling any emotion or enjoying anything in life. Many regularly stop taking the lithium, leading to the mood swings restarting. They search again for the feelings, the excitement and the thrill of the high.

............................

The first noticeable symptom of a manic episode is usually a deteriorating sleep pattern, staying up all night, too busy to sleep. One patient with a history of bipolar disorder on the long stay wards would start his escalation into mania by adding a hat to his daywear. He normally wore one hat. When he added a hat the notes would report, "now wearing two hats". This was the signal that all was not well, with the doctor being called. When he was seen wearing three hats it was usually time for his medication to include chlorpromazine. Balancing two hats was an art form. Three hats was usually a fashion mistake. The chlorpromazine would slowly lead to the hats reducing to two and then to one, back to comparative headwear normality.

# CHAPTER TWENTY SEVEN

Kenny, the other charge nurse on the ward, was gay. My books on "Psychiatric Nursing Studies", which were then a part of my reading habits, read now as if they were books from the Victorian era. The section on sexual psychiatry included chapters about "deviancy" that included homosexuality and it's treatments. But in the 1970s homosexuality seemed to be a non-issue and the idea of aversion therapy was, even then, something that was laughed at. Although St. Paul's could be "old school", Kenny was accepted totally by his peers. He was an old school charge nurse, and his "gayness" didn't prevent him fitting in with Bob, Jack and most of the others.

Aversion therapy, in the old sense, was rarely practiced in the asylum when I was there, although Kenny would tell of when he was involved in the procedure some years prior.

A 50 year old patient, Tim, had been admitted for assessment having been caught, on numerous occasions, by the police stealing underwear from the washing lines of the local community. The magistrates, tired of issuing a small fine, had referred him to the asylum for assessment and treatment. Two mornings a week he appeared in outpatients to be seen by an Eastern European psychiatrist. Kenny, a staff nurse at this stage, was assigned to help with outpatients and the psychiatrist had a word with him about Tim. The psychiatrist wanted to try aversion therapy for Tim's "knicker snatching". Kenny was therefore given a small amount of hospital funds and sent to the city to buy knickers, bras and suspender belts from a lingerie shop. Having embarrassingly bought these items, he returned to the psychiatrist who checked the sexy items and declared that he was pleased with the purchases.

A side room was set up with a chair, a bucket and a washing line (actually just string) tied between the window and a coat hook, with the lingerie items pegged out on the line. Tim was then given an injection to bring on vomiting and sent into the room for an hour. Obviously the idea was that the vomiting would take away his desire for the lingerie, a linkage between vomiting and lingerie would be more powerful psychologically than sex and lingerie. Kenny's task was to swab the room after Tim had completed his hour. The task was not pleasant as Tim's vomiting rarely hit the bucket which had been placed beside the chair. Having done this Kenny had to take down the lingerie, washing line and pegs, to store them in the administration office.

By the third treatment Kenny was unable to locate the lingerie items. Another lingerie fetishist had stolen them from the office, perhaps! The psychiatrist discharged Tim having been told that the hospital couldn't afford any more lingerie. So ended the aversion therapy for this fetishist.

Aversion therapy was also used, again generally unsuccessfully, in the treatment of alcoholics. When Peter told me about his depressing view of the "cure" rates for Ward 24, one of the least successful groups of patients were those with alcoholism. When an alcoholic was admitted they were usually given injections of a multi-vitamin drug, "Parentrovite". Along with this they also received a short course of anti-anxiety medication such as diazepam. They would be off the alcohol, staying on the ward for about three weeks, most of this time in pyjamas and dressing gown, to discourage them from absconding.

Opposite the road from the hospital was a large pub, The Cross Keys. It was to here, every weekday, that the charge nurses would visit on their way into, or out of, work. The Social Club only opened lunchtime at weekends. The Cross Keys had two public areas, a lounge bar and a public bar. The unwritten rule was that the lounge bar was for staff and the public bar for patients. Buying a pint, standing at the bar in the lounge, I was able to glimpse the public bar area. Therefore it was with a feeling of pleasure that I regularly spotted one or two of my old patients from Ward 2. But along with Charlie and his mates would often be another one or two patients in dressing gowns and pyjamas. Being inappropriately dressed was no barrier to getting a drink. These "dressing gowns" were from the acute wards.

I asked Peter about the drug "Antabuse". This drug, which had been around since the 1960s, was given to alcoholics who, if they then drank alcohol, would be violently sick. It was another of the aversion therapies. I asked Peter why this drug was never given on the Ward 24. "Why would anyone give Antabuse?" he asked, waiting for me to show my ignorance. The best teachers always threw questions back as questions for the questioner.

"Cos, once they've had the Antabuse they can't drink," was my response.

"Who said they couldn't?"

"The School of Nursing. They said if it was given, it'd make them very sick."

"They're right about that. It makes them vomit. Look," said Peter with a sigh, "if they want to give up alcohol, they will. Mostly they don't want to, but they want to look as if they do. You'll see them all over at The Cross Keys. They still manage to wander there, even in their pyjamas. We check them for bottles of alcohol on admission, so the only place for them to get their booze is The Cross Keys."

"But if they had Antabuse, then if they got over to The Cross Keys, they wouldn't be able to drink."

"Who told you they couldn't drink on Antabuse? Course they can drink, they still drink, but throw up, then return to the drink and throw up again. All the Antabuse does is make them throw up. So you'll have the vomit to clear up as well. When the Antabuse was given out the patients would still come over here, but the landlord would complain about how much vomit he'd had to clear up. If you were from that ward, he'd make you help. No point in Antabuse. Useless."

The treatment for alcoholism on Ward 24 was accepted as being a short, often a very short, period of abstinence after which they returned to either illicit drinking of spirits on the ward, or were discharged to start the drinking process again at home. The admission was almost always due to someone else, the courts, the family or the spouse giving them "one last chance", and the patient agreed to the admission. Once the admission had failed they were then able to argue that they had done their bit, and everything then returned to the depressing status quo.

Ward 24 had one particularly odd admission during my time as a student nurse. A man had been sectioned on a Friday night having been found in a state of collapse. Due to his responses at the scene, he was taken back to the police station and was seen by a police surgeon. His hallucinated and deluded clinical picture suggested that this was someone who needed an assessment, and so he was sectioned, unceremoniously put back into an ambulance and placed in a side room of St. Paul's. His admitting doctor saw him around 3am, but couldn't even make out his name, due to the semi-comatose nature of the new arrival. It was decided that the 48-hour section should remain.

The following morning he awoke. The patient couldn't believe his situation. He was, in fact, a student nurse, at present in his third year, in the same group as Ron, having just started working on that very ward. He was initially on nights. He'd been off sick with a tooth infection, been put onto "Metronidazole", an antibiotic, had been in the city having a few too many drinks, and this medication in conjunction with the alcohol had done for him. It took until late that day for him to be assessed by a psychiatrist and discharged off his section. The School of Nursing gave him a warning for this behaviour. His response was to enquire if he was entitled to overtime for the long period he'd spent on his ward!

My acute experience was coming to an end. Thinking it through I couldn't help but feel that Peter had defined the acute experience better than the School of Nursing. The expectations of "cure" didn't materialise. Unlike the long stay or geriatric experience I had spent too much time wondering who was ill, who was an addict requiring but not receiving specialist treatment, and who was just trying to get off a criminal conviction. Those who definitely were ill, with an obvious psychiatric diagnosis, were generally patched up with a recognition that they would be coming back to visit soon. The only exception to this rule, during my first acute experience, was the student nurse.

# CHAPTER TWENTY-EIGHT

"I particularly asked for you to be my student nurse. I need you to take me to a car park."

Deb, my community psychiatric nurse, CPN, had only just picked me up from the Nurses Home. As she drove towards the city she made the first of those remarks that caused me to love her. It was a remark without introduction. The statement was left hanging. There was no obvious response. Statements from Deb usually had an apparent rootlessness. The secret was in tracing back her thinking, finding the roots, then giving an answer. It was a whole new type of conversation. Deb continued to drive her ten-year-old Ford Fiesta, very slowly, the traffic collecting in a long queue behind us. As I considered the statement I realised that she was still in second gear. Should I mention this? I soon learned to be careful about criticism towards Deb. She was as wily and unpredictable as Agatha Christie's Miss Marple.

In reality Deborah had probably drawn the short straw by getting me as her student nurse. Middle-aged with permed short hair, a pleated skirt, cardigan and brogues, she was as fashionable as a fifties soap opera, but who was I to judge, I who couldn't even wear appropriate shoes. I initially dreaded the weeks ahead with her. It'd be like doing the job with my mother alongside. This was to change on that first journey.

"So, what's this about a car park?" I considered this a safe open response to her odd statement.

"When I was asked who I wanted to come round with me, I told the School of Nursing I wanted you. I knew you were quite young. I also knew you had a scooter. So I knew you'd be able to take me to a car park." The logic still didn't quite make sense. But there was a seed of logic somewhere, if I could find it.

"Why, of all things, a car park?"

"I've never been to a car park. You know, one of those ones with lots of floors, in a building. I knew you'd know about them, so you could take me, and I'd know what to do if I ever needed to park there."

"Right. When were you thinking of this outing?"

Deb looked straight at me. "Now, of course." With that simple response she continued, still in second gear, to the city. As we drove I now had so many questions to ask. If Deb hadn't experienced a car park, what else could I show her? I might be more important than the lowly student I generally felt I was. That one trip to town told me everything I needed to know. Deb was a country girl now hitting her 50s. She was not too proud to ask me to get her "up to speed" on certain important things in life, such as car parks, things she never dared ask her spouse or children.

The drive to the car park threw up more gems of life as seen from Deb's perspective. I asked her about family, two grown up sons both in the car repair business. The engine was screaming to be put into top gear, rather than the second gear she insisted on.

I stared at the gear-stick, but without reaction from Deb. "…might be worth changing up a gear, I can't really hear you that well."

"My sons always tell me I don't use the gears properly, but it goes as fast as I want it to and, as I'm alone for most of the time, the noise doesn't bother me." There was no answer to that. It was her car; she could drive how she wanted. My mind wandered. We were now stuck in traffic. Deb revved the car constantly as we waited for something to move.

After a few moments of silence, ".....and they also keep on telling me I'm not filling up my car battery in the proper way," she said plaintively.

I tried to keep up with the line of thinking. "Who?"

"My sons, of course."

I decided to give some of my almost non-existent pearls of wisdom to this car servicing discussion. "They say a battery needs to have distilled water just over the elements, no more than that, and needs to be checked regularly to make certain the elements are still just covered," I replied, trying to sound as if, like most men, I knew something about vehicle maintenance.

"Yes. That's what they keep telling me." Again, a long pause. "I suppose they're experts with cars. They are mechanics. I'm not. Perhaps I should follow their advice." Another pause. "But they regularly have new cars and replace their batteries every couple of years. I fill my battery up to the top every time and it's the same battery that came with the car. That's ten years ago. It's never let me down."

It was silly to preach to Deb. She was much wiser than me.

Having shown her the complicated entry and exit of a multi-storey car park she was delighted. "I don't think I'll ever use it. I never really come into the city. But I do feel grand about having the ability to use it if I want to, and to tell my sons I've been in one. They'll be really surprised."

We set out for the small villages in the north of the county, her round for the day. I asked if she'd always covered this patch. "Always. This is where I grew up and where I live today. It's been my home forever. I'll never understand why anyone would want to go anywhere else."

"So where do you go on your holidays?" I asked.

"I don't. Holidays are days off work, so I muddle around at home doing jobs that need doing, looking after the chickens, doing a bit of gardening." She thought for a moment. "Wait a minute. I did go to the seaside once, but didn't like it. Have you lived round here for long?"

"No. I was born here but since then have lived in Derbyshire and South Wales. Now I'm back again."

Deb looked genuinely askance at this amount of change of scenery. "You're very well travelled. I don't know how you cope with all the moving and getting used to a new place." I was, to Deb, almost as daring as Captain Scott.

Still not sure I was hearing this right, I pushed further. "You've been to London I suppose?"

"London? I don't think I've ever been out of the county." She suddenly slapped the steering wheel. "Yes I have. Of course I have. Silly of me to forget. I once went just over the border to transfer a patient. That must be the only time."

Deb was basically a wonderful home bird, doing a thankless task, who seemed so full of happiness for the simple things in life, whilst trying to keep up with just enough modernity to survive.

In the late 1970s the role of the CPN was primarily to administer depot injections to people. I became aware that, in all my time as a student nurse, this was the first time that patients were considered people, rather than patients. The depot injections, these long acting anti-psychotic medications, kept the patients, not necessarily well, but at least out of the asylum. These injections were a fortnightly link to a professional who could make a cursory assessment of their progress or otherwise.

Working in the hospital provided the backup needed if the situation got sticky. In the community the nurse was in the patients' territory. In the leafy meandering patch of Deb's, that territory could be somewhat odd, as I was to find out.

I gradually recognised that with Deb directing me for the next three months there would be excitement as well as novelty. It was great to be out of the asylum environment for a while. I also recognised that the long distances travelled through the lovely villages would be very slowly eaten up, in second gear!

.......................................

Although four days a week I would be totally with Deb, for one day I was given one or two people to visit. These people were not considered difficult. They were people who needed company as well as observation.

"You'll take over Percy, for the time being. You know him from Ward 7. He was in when you were there, so you're someone he knows as well. He'll like having a man to discuss "man things" with. I'll continue to see him but you'll do the ongoing work." In a funny way I now had my own patient, someone I saw alone, someone for whom I was, or felt, responsible.

We drove to a northern suburb of the city. Once introduced it was to be my role to visit each week. Deb was realistic about my usefulness. "You'll now be his visitor, keeping an eye on him on a weekly basis. He'll love it when you arrive on your moped. He's into machines. He'll want to talk about gadgets and electrics." I knew nothing about either.

Percy lived in a small three-roomed bungalow. Whether by design or luck, the bungalow was almost directly opposite the road from the doctors surgery, so it was here that Deb took me first. She had worked this patch for long enough to know the staff in that surgery well, especially the practice nurse, Joy. Between Joy and Deb they provided all the systems for ensuring that Percy was safe, fed and well. I was to make this duo a trio, for better or worse. Joy had been the district nurse for that surgery for most of her professional life. She knew her patients and had often known their parents before them. She and the surgery were family practitioners in more than name.

Percy was waiting for me. Small, almost bald, with glasses that looked as if they had come straight from the 1948 Beveridge National Health Service collection, he ushered me in. He had little small talk. We sat in the lounge, Percy looking out of the window, me looking at Percy. Although he remembered me, Percy, a delight in Ward 7, where the competition wasn't great given the very high percentage of patients with advanced dementia, was not a natural conversationalist. A private man, he was a reluctant friend, knowing that this "friend" was there to check on him. He knew he was in a disadvantage in this forced duet.

The inside was basic, clean, and functional. The furniture looked as if it had been bought from second hand dealers, post war utility. The two easy chairs didn't match and neither did the two chairs next to the very small dining table.

British Aerospace had been Percy's work since his successful apprenticeship. Fascinated by machinery all his life Percy was thrilled to work for such a company, a vanguard of engineering. Yet Percy worked in administration, completing paperwork far away from the exciting arm of development and research. Put in a requisition for fan blades. Percy wouldn't be involved. Put in a requisition for toilet rolls and Percy's your man! This, of course, didn't dampen his enthusiasm for high tech. His particular specialism was radios, of all sorts, as long as they were crystal sets! Dotted round his lounge, crystal sets of all types took pride of place on shelves and tables. From these, wires were strung around the room, quite tidily, but something of a garrote to the unwary. Central to the room was a 1970s stereogram, a lumbering oak effect chest with a large lid, into which records were played. The lid was now was stained with circles, from the hot mugs of coffee left on it, looking like a wayward Olympic logo by Andy Warhol. This stereogram provided Percy with the news he was both fascinated and frustrated by. It also allowed him to listen to the radio without the need for an earpiece, the only way of hearing his crystal sets.

Percy's other interest was trade union history. Coming from a socialist background, he had dabbled in everything from communism to Marxism, but now settled himself as a main stream Labour Party supporter. In the past he occasionally attended trades union meetings and conferences, but when the "loony left" started to move Labour from working class to a radicalised intellectual position, he lost much interest. He would still talk politics; he no longer lived politics.

Unmarried, Percy had probably found his soul mates in either the union or his work, but now he was lonely and isolated. His radios were his only company.

Percy had started his more severe depressions whilst still at British Aerospace. After a number of admissions he took early retirement from the company when he was only fifty. With work gone his slide into even more severe depressive phases increased. Sitting alone in his small bungalow he found that even his radios failed to connect him to others of a like mind. Once he'd been a member of a radio society who met every week, swapping stories and bits of radio with each other. This was now past. He was clinging to crystal radios when others had let go. He was a Crystal Radio Society of one!

Joy had close contact with Percy, not only working opposite his house but also living round the corner. Percy's depressions seemed to have a known cycle, one that Joy, Deb and gradually myself came to recognise. A trigger would set him on an initial downward slide. The trigger could be something he'd heard on his stereogram, or something he'd thought about overnight. The trigger led to further negative thoughts, which would put him back to bed. Covered with a duvet he ruminated, finding all the negatives of his, and others, lives, which would transport him to a place of even greater worthlessness. He became bedridden where he felt safest.

It was usually at this stage that Joy, or perhaps Deb, would find him, not eating, covered up in bed, tearful. Percy would be moved to Ward 7, where Barbara, the psychiatrist and Jack and his team would recommence their work, which would lead to his discharge. Initially this route was circumvented by his refusal to open the door. He wouldn't get out of bed to allow the visitor in. Joy had discussed this with Percy at a time when he was brighter, with Percy agreeing to having a duplicate front door key for those terrible occasions. This key was held at the doctor's surgery for emergencies.

The psychiatrist, Barbara, was involved in this "care package", giving permission for an "open door" policy when it came to Percy. If he needed admission the normal route of district nurse to CPN to GP to psychiatrist could be shortened. If Percy was poorly, get him admitted; the paperwork could wait. Oh for such flexibility nowadays.

So it was that Percy was one of the first people I was introduced to as a student nurse under Deb. Once a week I would visit, have a cup of tea, talk politics and radios, and check he was taking his anti-depressants, before leaving. I would do this throughout my time with Deb, right up to Christmas, the end of this experience and the end of my training.

So, as I sat there opposite Percy I asked him about his work, his interests and his house. Percy rarely left the house, apart from watering a few sorry plants in his back yard. His contacts were Joy, who visited every couple of days, Deb, who visited every fortnight and now me. He visited the local shop for his needs, but Percy's needs were few. I tried to encourage Percy to get out for a walk with me but, without any enthusiasm, the offer was never grasped. Percy was as content as he could be having his "cuppa", whilst talking about what he'd heard on the radio. He would talk about the crystal sets, but the electronics knowledge required from me was too much, so politics and his past occupation at British Aerospace were as far as I could ever get. With no family, no friends and no communal activities he'd agree to, he chose a minimalist lifestyle.

Once a week he was content, but not necessarily happy, to have a student nurse for a cup of tea. I realised, after a couple of sessions with Percy that I had to mug up on crystal sets. The conversation wasn't easy. My knowledge of British Aerospace, British socialism of the 50s and crystal radio sets wasn't fluent enough to maintain a conversation for an hour.

# CHAPTER TWENTY-NINE

Injections given in a clinic, took place in semi-sterile surroundings. Injections in peoples' houses presented far greater challenges.

Carl was a young man with a short history of schizophrenia. As we pulled up at the terraced house in one of the villages Deb told me I would be administering the injection. By this time I felt confident that I could jab with the best. Bounding out of the house with a huge smile for Deb, Carl was brought up short by my presence. The smile vanished. Deb was his; third parties were not welcome.

"Who is ............THIS?" he snapped. Deb brushed off the aggressive posturing.

"Why, this is Stuart," said Deb brightly, aware that all was far from well. "He's going to be a nurse, just like me. I'm teaching him, so I told that he just had to meet you! That's why he's here. I thought you'd be pleased to see a man for a change."

The bullshit didn't work; even Carl could see through it. "He's not doing anything to me, not anything. He's not invited here. He's not fucking welcome. He can't come in. He'll be dead if he steps through that door. He's probably been sent to snoop on me!" Carl turned to me, prodding me with a finger. "You........ Get back in the fucking car. Never come back or I'll kill you!" His eyes narrowed as he leant towards me. I could smell a mixture of stale cigarettes and icy hatred. "I know all about you. You've been watching me, wising me up. Well, it stops now! Fuck off!"

Undeterred, Deb stepped in, "I just wanted Stuart to do your injection. That's all."

"No fucking way. He'll put something in it. He's dangerous. He's got two seconds to get back in the car or I'll rip his fucking head off. Only you do my injection – only you!"

"Carl, sometimes I can't get here. What happens when I'm away on holiday?" Given that Deb was never away on holiday this was something of a bluff.

"Then the injection dun't 'appen. That's what! Either you do it, or it don't get fucking done!"

I got back in the car, not needing to be told twice. If he didn't like me, or didn't want me there, then I had no intention of coming to grief at the hands of an 'aggressive, psychotic, maniac'.

Deb and Carl went inside.

Ten minutes later she returned, got in and we drove away. On the way back to the hospital I studied her carefully. She turned and smiled, "Carl can be a bit of a scallywag at times, but normally he's absolutely lovely."

What could I say? She had just rewritten the Oxford English Dictionary.

..........................

Deb realised that she needed to contact patients before dropping in with student nurse attached. Many patients didn't like the imposition of such a useless character in their regular visits. So it was that Deb, on her fortnightly visit to a remote farm, had asked permission for me to accompany her to the house of Bill and

Cyril, two brothers living "in the sticks". They had, probably reluctantly, agreed. They trusted Deb, who was cock-a-hoop. It was the first time that they had allowed anyone to accompany her.

"Please - no comments until later!"

The by-roads were twisting and narrow. Once off these we drove for some distance on an un-tarmaced road, before turning onto a muddy track. After grinding along in first gear for what felt like an age, the house finally came into view. Driving with Deb was always slow progress.

From a distance the house looked special, two stories, old, with a lovely eight windowed façade, a dilapidated barn on one side and a large garage on the other. Pulling up outside the front door it didn't live up to first impressions. Some windows were boarded over, many of the frames were rotten and the porch was missing a main strut to hold up the roof, which now sagged to the right. As we entered we needed to dip our heads. A once fancy bell chain hung by the front door, but the top of the chain dangled uselessly from its spacer, which was no longer connected. Although there was glazing in the door, it was blackened both by age and lack of cleaning. Very little light could pass through it. Deb knocked firmly. Cyril opened the door.

The aroma was more apparent than the person. It was the smell of newly spread slurry, a smell so strong that I instinctively reached to my jacket pocket for a mint. Anything to assuage my olfactory senses. As we moved through the house the smell, rather than diminishing, grew worse. Should I breathe through my mouth or nose? Could I take really shallow breaths? Could I actually hold my breath?

Deb had told me at length about the two brothers, Cyril and Bill. Living with farming parents, Cyril, the elder son, was expected to inherit the farm. The second son, William, had not been well for as long as anyone could remember, suffering with chronic schizophrenia. Both had been regular truants at school. The parents had plucked them permanently from the classroom as soon as they legally could.

As their parents aged, Cyril had split his time between caring for them and for an increasingly disturbed Bill. Less and less time was spent working the farm. Unworked farms quickly revert to nature.

Their parents had been dead for at least ten years. The farm had rapidly slid into a decay that mirrored the disintegration in Bill's mind. Cyril had struggled to combine care for Bill with tending the large mixed farm. Everyone had suffered until Cyril sold the land, just holding onto the house, which had been in the family for three generations. The money from the sale was secreted around the house in large bundles of cash, growing as mouldy as the rest of the decor. Cyril didn't trust the banks.

Their parents had probably hoped for one of them to marry, bringing new blood to the family farm, but this hope never had a chance. As I moved through the house I quickly realised that no young woman would be tempted by a property such as this. There would be simply no future in it.

Cyril now cared for his younger brother as best he could. He had been a hard-working farmer, but he had never grasped the skills of cooking, cleaning and tidying. The first sight of the inside of the house confirmed his distinct limitations. The heat. The smell. The decay.

At least my arrival was not unexpected. Visitors were unwelcome. Unexpected visitors were an active threat. During the last local elections a County Councillor, visiting to ask for their vote, had been seen off with a shotgun.

The hall was a dark cavern, though I was aware of objects and boxes and smells. We turned right into the main lounge. The centre of the lounge had a table strewn with bits of soggy paper, empty mugs and odd pieces of machinery – farm or household? I had no idea. All the paper on the table was brown, discoloured and damp. Spots of yellow-brown speckled the debris.

I was there to give Bill his injection but the lounge presented so many questions. What to say? What to do? Why is it like this? I stood by the table, unsure of myself. The usual statements of "lovely house" or "what pretty wallpaper" were of no use. I could usually find a positive phrase but was completely stumped on this occasion. We stood in silence, Deb beside me watching my reaction. I was aware, in the silence, of a dull hum, quiet but persistent. Was it a generator or an electric fan?  The room was so dark. Windows by the table were only partly visible, the old brown curtains letting through only a crack of light.

"Can I draw the curtains a bit to give us some light?" Deb asked.

"Mmmm," grunted Cyril.

I could sense him thinking. "Why?  Just need to be closed later."

Deb moved to the curtains, pulled them slightly apart, letting light into the lounge. As she did so a swarm of flies took off, buzzing around. It was the noise I had heard, I thought, but it had been coming from the other door. What was through there? Deb gave me her briefcase, which I set down on the table. Inside were

Bill's notes, to be completed after the injection. I opened the case and placed the notes on the table.

As I did so Bill came through the door from behind which the buzzing seemed loudest. Initially he looked like Cyril, but it was obvious that, although younger than his brother, he was in a disturbed state. The schizophrenia had taken its toll. He had some tremors of his arms as well as the usual tardive dyskinesia - the stretching jaw and mouth, the side effect of his medication. Bill was insecure. He didn't look at us at all, just stared at his brother for reassurance.

They both had shoulder length hair, not from fashion but refusal to pay a barber. It was unkempt and probably un-brushed since childhood. Both also had beards. Both had few teeth, tooth stumps protruding alarmingly in all directions. Despite this both seemed well nourished and both had a good colour.

They wore lace-up boots (though Bill's were unlaced), thick cloth trousers of a colour determined by their long history of messy eating, open necked shirts (buttons missing), and all topped off by aged sports jackets, much torn and food smeared. I wondered if they took off their jackets at bedtime. Perhaps. They seemed never to have changed these clothes; the outfits were held together by the decaying food. Wash them and they'd disintegrate. Like the farm .... like Bill.

Deb had told me on the journey up that a few months before Cyril, whilst wandering outside, had fallen into some discarded machinery and broken his ankle. He had allowed Deb to see it. She had been shocked by the obvious fracture, but Cyril refused outright to go to hospital. He'd never been near a hospital in his life and wild horses wouldn't get him there now, whatever the crisis. His solution had been to find some string to bind his boots tight. "It'll get better in time," he'd muttered, which it did. He still walked with a definite limp, but the tight boots provided a type of plaster cast until healing had occurred naturally. He hadn't taken off the boots since the accident, Deb assumed.

Cyril moved back towards the hall, away from the lounge area, if it could be called that. I briefly opened the case holding the syringes and other paraphernalia of injections. I motioned to Deb.

"Where can I wash my hands?"

Knowing that Bill was standing there listening she mouthed, "forget it."

"Jab me in the bedroom," Bill snapped, turned and left the room. His bedroom? What shocks lay up there?

I closed the briefcase. Bill had already gone. Leaving the notes on the table I followed Deb through the door taking a sharp right turn to climb the very steep bare stairs. I was about to follow Deb but there were two doors in that hallway, both ajar. My curiosity was overwhelming. The stench was now almost overpowering; the mint had been sucked to oblivion. I pushed open the first door seeing, with the quickest of glances, a washbasin. The downstairs toilet. No interest there. Yet, as I pulled the door back the flies swarmed again. What was in there? I poked my head around the door.

What I discovered was a Turner Prize winning sculpture. This was what the flies were swarming around. The toilet itself, almost invisible to the eye, had no seat. Forming a pyramid that reached almost to the top of the cistern, an inverted ice-cream cone of excrement pointed skywards. The turds had obviously accumulated over ..... who knows, but the result was that the only possible way for the brothers to have been able to use the toilet would have involved an intricate personal ballet, feet placed either side of the toilet rim, backside just above the height of the existing volcano. At times this ballet had clearly failed and either the excrement or one of the brothers had slid off the top to drop on the floor. Smudges, skid-marks and nodules of semi-trodden excrement covered either side of the basin. And there was no loo paper! Tracey Emin might have been proud of this work of art; certainly the flies were.

I was needed upstairs but could not resist just checking the other unseen room. Pushing open this door, knowing that I was also pushing my luck, I investigated. It was the kitchen, but unlike any kitchen that I had ever seen before: meals-on-wheels foil trays scattered everywhere; lumps of green and rotten meat moulded around what I eventually realised was an electric stove; plates piled on every surface, including the floor, all furry with meat and food remains, and wires, some bare, connected appliances that clearly hadn't worked for years. Were the wires bare because the appliances didn't work, or vice versa?

Pulling the door to, I scampered up the stairs.

"Sorry for the delay. I forgot the alcohol swabs," I lied.

Bill lay on his side on the bed, his scrawny bottom a dim glow in the darkness. As elsewhere, the curtains were closed, but a little light seeped through their stained and fading folds. Even here the aroma was acrid, nauseating, strong enough to make me cough or retch. Here the stench was mostly of urine, though other smells lingered in the background, smells of an unknown origin. Smells that I would rather not identify. I kept my breathing as shallow as I could. There were some questions I didn't want answered.

I drew up the medication. His trousers were already round his ankles. I looked for the swab realising suddenly that, despite my excuse, I had forgotten to put them in the briefcase at the start of the day. The level of filth in the room suggested that wiping the area would only spread it further. To be in the correct position for giving the jab, I had to rest one knee on the bed.

A moment later the injection was finished. I tapped Bill. "All done, you can pull your trousers up now." As I lifted my knee I became aware of the sogginess. My knee and calf were drenched; I knew why. As if I hadn't already realised, the bedroom, dark, filthy and stinking, finally confirmed that no woman would ever be prepared to bring in the new blood so desperately needed to make their house a home.

Deb and I returned to the lounge. I had to sign that the injection had been administered. I also needed to make notes on the visit, but decided to do both later, in the car, where the air was cleaner. My notes were now speckled with yellow-brown spots. We'd only been upstairs for a few minutes. Where had these appeared from? I glanced upward. The grey/black ceiling had globules of fluid hanging, suspended. I placed the briefcase on the table to put the notes away. To the left was a slightly open drawer. The three or four inch gap was enough to see that inside were ten pound notes, not one or two, but rolls and rolls of them. I didn't stop to question either Cyril or Bill.

I left, preceding Deb, politely saying thank you to the brothers who were already disappearing.

Sitting alongside Deb in the Fiesta I tried to understand what I had seen.

"Why are they allowed to live there?"

"Why?" Deb replied.

Realising I had to be careful, I thought for a moment before continuing.

"Surely in this day and age they shouldn't be allowed to live like that?" I stopped. Surely "surely" implied that it might not be "surely". I was getting into deep water.

"Why?" repeated Deb.

"It's not good for them, it'll make them sick."

"Who says it makes them sick? Were they sick today?" Another long pause. Deb was forcing me to think through this complex ethical conundrum. "Check through my notes. The thing about the brothers is that they are so rarely sick. I'll bet you and I have had more colds and flu in a year than they've had in five, or even ten. So, what's the issue?"

"Have you seen the toilet?" I left the question open, not telling her yet of the inverted cone of turds.

"Yes. It's a bit of a pickle, isn't it?" She stopped the car, pulling into a lay-by. "What would you do about it?"

"Get the Council in to clear it for a start."

"They refuse all help. The last Council staff to attend was welcomed with a twelve bore. I'm about the only one they'll accept, although now, perhaps, you're accepted as well. You see .... if I, or we, pull out, they'll have no one. They could be collected by the police, taken to a safe place, assessed by a psychiatrist but the end result would be that even if they were considered a risk to others, which I don't think they necessarily are, they would be sectioned under the Mental Health Act, taken to the asylum for assessment but soon released. And then who'd visit them? Nobody, 'cause after that they'd never agree to a visit. They'd feel betrayed. Mentally Bill is as good as he'll ever be. I've visited them for eight years. I've always managed to get medication into Bill. I've got them meals-on-wheels, which they eat, even if they don't tidy up afterwards. Like most people who have made a choice of lifestyles, they won't be changed by force. In the community we work to try to keep people out of hospital, as well as safe. Cyril and Bill aren't easy, but at least they let us in."

With that Deb reached for her Tupperware lunch pot, snapped off the top and nibbled on a sandwich. How she could eat following that? The smell was still over all my clothes. My leg was now cold, but still quite damp. My every breath took me back into that house.

I thought about all this. My own limited experience told me that I couldn't live the way that these brothers did. But, at the same time, no one was asking me to. I reached for the notes. At least I could sign that the injection had been administered. As I signed I noticed the spots on it. "Deb, what was it dripping onto the table?"

"Never mind," said Deb. "I'm working on it."

"Working on what?"

"Well.... Bill is very incontinent. Don't know why, he refuses to see the doctor, but he's been like it for years. Each night he drenches the bed. The mattress is sodden. It drips through the floor and ceiling, into the lounge."

"Well, at least I now know why my knee was soggy and why there were spots on the notes. Can't anything be done to get him sorted – a new mattress, commode by the bed....... something?" I was still looking for simple solutions. Clearly Deb had also come up with these short-term solutions some time back, which she now confessed to.

"Some years ago I had this brainwave," said Deb with her usual honesty. "Bill refused a new mattress. The urine was still coming through the ceiling into the lounge, but I'd noticed a large old tin bath, lying in the shed, probably used on the farm at some stage to feed the cattle. I persuaded Bill that this could be strategically placed under the bed to catch the urine. At least it would stop it dripping onto them, and me."

"Brilliant idea Deb." I sat there thinking.   "But the urine's still coming through the ceiling?"

"I know. I can't yet work out an answer to it. For about two years the flow of urine stopped. The problem is, I hadn't worked out what to do with the tin bath once it was full. It's been full for about 6 months. It's too heavy to move. The urine now just trickles over the edge. Bill still won't allow me to get the Council in. I can't lower the level of urine 'cause I can't get under the bed to scoop it out with a bucket. But neither can I move the bath, it's far too heavy. And I can't move the bed either. And, on top of that, I now worry whether the massive weight of the full tin bath might cause the ceiling to collapse. It's a bit of a problem. I'm working on it."

I could see it was "a bit of a problem" and I had no magic solution. Over the years I, like others who worked the community patches, found that so many people were so different in so many different ways. To impose society's values on individuals and families was often of little worth. People could be very odd or very ill, or both. Banging them up in asylums never was, and never is, a good idea. It can only be a last resort.

I often wonder what happened to the brothers. I have no idea. I fear that at some later stage, as they grew older, the police, social workers and the local council would have gone in, removed the brothers and placed them in care, where they would have simply faded away. Although I struggled to breathe in that farmhouse, for the brothers it was their home. Forcibly evicted from their home, they would quite simply die.

I looked forward to returning to Percy, his nice cuppa tea. There would be no drips to watch out for there. Percy's case was simple and straightforward. That was some consolation, at least.

# CHAPTER THIRTY

Things can unravel in the community with amazing rapidity. So it was that the following week I dropped in on Percy, just before lunch on my one day a week when I was working on my own. I had been in the library that morning working on an essay. I tried to ensure that my visits to Percy were around this time, the same time every week.

I knew things were not right when I first got there. Percy was a gentleman of an older order, so even though this was my fourth visit to him, I was following his routines, picking up the rules of his lifestyle. Each time I arrived he would be keeping an eye out for me, ready at the door, kettle boiled.

But there was no sign of Percy as I stood on the doorstep. I sensed something was wrong. I knocked on the door. No response. I walked to the back of the house, careful not to knock over the plant pots. Further knocks on the backdoor still brought no answer. I knew he was in. He was always in.

Luckily the district nurse, Joy, across the road at the doctor's surgery, was in. I explained the situation. Joy reported that she'd seen Percy that morning, although he'd seemed quiet and evasive. Reaching into her top drawer she took out a key. "Deb and I had this cut, with Percy's permission, for when he took to his bed. He'll probably need to go to Ward 7, but see what you think."

"Can I use your phone?"

"Of course." I phoned Barbara to confirm that I could get Percy into Ward 7 if needed. I also called Deb, leaving her a message, before re-crossing the road clutching Percy's front door key.

Knocking again on the door, still produced no response. I turned the key in the lock and entered. The front room was empty. "Hi Percy. It's just me, Stuart," I called. No answer. I went through to the bedroom. Percy was in bed, curtains closed, curled up under his bedclothes.

"Sorry. Just feel awful. No reason to get up. Leave me alone and I'll be OK. I'm wasting everyone's time," he said feebly.

"Percy. Don't apologise. It's one of those things. You get down every so often. It's not the first or the last. It's one of your depressions. Are you OK about going into hospital, just to get you right?"

"....think I'll have to. Can't face things at the moment. Sorry ......so useless."

I needed to get a move on.

With that I went back to Joy who organised for an ambulance to get Percy to Ward 7. I returned to sit with Percy, collecting enough clothes and sundries to keep him going. Once the ambulance arrived I saw Percy into it before returning again to Joy to phone the ward, warning of his impending arrival.

I sat chatting with Joy, having gone as far as I could with Percy for now. Jack and his team would take good care of him, at least making sure he received his medication along with three good meals a day. Deb would be the main link liaising with the various professionals involved.

Joy and Deb both had the same outlook on life, with a good sense of humour but seriousness about their own work. We talked of our experiences, hers long, mine short. "I don't know how you can keep sane with all those people you visit," she remarked. "You must be a saint." I tried to dispel any saintly comparisons, aware that Joy and Deb were much more saintly and forbearing than I was. I also remembered that the decision to go into mental health nursing was certainly not due to saintliness, but more to the need for a quick job. Oh, then there were the shoes.

"How about spending your next day off with me? You can come on my rounds and advise me." I agreed to this. New experiences were always welcome for me. But advising Joy? I wasn't sure what advice I could give her.

..................................

The following week I sat with Joy in her Escort holding, on my knee, a much larger case than I was used to. With Deb there were just a few syringes and needles to carry, whereas Joy had what I considered was almost enough to carry out open-heart surgery. Joy had one particular visit to make that morning which she thought might be of interest to me. She also genuinely believed I might have some suggestions to make about the patient we were to see.

Living alone in a bungalow Martha was a middle-aged woman with a problem. Joy had been visiting her for about a year, but could find no obvious method to improve the outcome. Every district nurse gets frustrated by particular patients on their books. Some district nurses are adept at discharging these patients and moving them on. Others seem to keep patients on their books forever, watching over them, until a bright idea comes round. Joy was hoping I'd be that bright idea.

The bungalow smelled of dead meat. I squeezed in next to Martha after the introductions. I use the word squeezed, as I was unable to find a space large enough for my bottom. A sofa and easy chair were the only two places available. Joy had taken the easy chair, opposite Martha, so I had no option but to try to find a few inches of space alongside the patient. Martha was enormous. She was so corpulent that her gigantic form almost entirely filled the three-seater settee. Rolls of her seemed to flow everywhere. In physics I'd read that each mass changes all other masses; Martha's certainly did.

Joy leant forward, unpacking her case. Bits of equipment, bags, bottles and sterile packs soon littered the floor around Martha's feet. Joy was to dress Martha's leg ulcers. I'd never seen a leg ulcer before so was excited, in a childish sort of a way. I joined in the light chatter, mostly around what had been on TV last night, but my thoughts were driven by what was under the bandages covering both legs.

As Joy peeled away the bandages, it felt to me like an old fashioned game of pass-the-parcel; each layer removed heightened my expectations. As the layers were removed, so the smell increased. As each layer was removed they became ever more soggy and soaked with blood and puss. Before long the floor was adorned with an obscene pile of discarded bandages. At last the legs were revealed. What legs! Both oozed blood, seeping from many unseen wells beneath. Some areas of the legs were black, some white, and some greeny-yellow. Each leg, although huge, was massively distorted. Large indentations, some caused by bandaging, some by tissue loss, reminded me of the layered tiles on a roof. Even as I watched the oozing of the blood increased, blotting out more and more of the yellow and white tissue, making the leg resemble a multi-coloured candy stick. After cleaning both legs with saline the new dressings, sticky bandages, were applied by Joy, followed by a tubular bandage. The cause of the massive ulceration was poor blood supply through Martha's legs. This was caused by Martha's enormous weight, leading to her lack of mobility.

Back in the car we drove on to her next appointment. On the way Joy explained the problem. "She's so huge. I need to get her weight down, but I'm not succeeding. She's over twenty-five stone, so I have to take her to a weighbridge each month to see how much she's losing. It's the only place where people weighing that much can be measured. Her weight has been creeping up as long as I've known her. I gave her advice about what to eat and drew up plans for gentle exercise. But nothing worked. She can only walk a few steps now, just enough to get to the kitchen. As she becomes more immobile, so her weight increases."

"Have you got the experts from the general hospital in on the act?" I asked.

"I've had everyone bar the chief executive involved: dieticians, physicians, physiotherapists and occupational therapists. The family have also been involved, though they weren't much help. We had meetings which eventually led to a measured diet being delivered each day, all labelled, everything she needs for survival, but also for reducing weight. The cost is huge but we all know that this is her last chance. If we can get a few stone off her, then we can get her to a day centre a few days a week, where she can have more active physio'. The special diet started two month ago but it's not working."

"Why?"

"I took her to the weigh-bridge the week before last. She'd put on an additional stone. There's a meeting next week with all the professionals. They'll want answers. I have none. I've checked. She's having her diet."

"Do you visit her every week?"

"Yeah, every Friday, like today."

"Do you always visit at the same time?"

"Yeah, ten o'clock, it's my first visit after doing my admin."

"Can we go back now? It's almost midday. I'd like to see her again. And not at her regular time. We could say we have dropped in because you think you've left your glasses down the side of the easy chair. We might just find out something to explain the weight gain."

"Okay, let's do it," Joy resignedly said, but without much enthusiasm.

Back at Martha's house we knocked at the door and let ourselves in. Martha never answered the door herself, saving her energy for getting to the toilet instead. Joy shouted, "Hi there, it's only Joy again."

Entering the lounge it was obvious that we were disturbing lunch. Sitting with Martha was her daughter. A plateful of burgers and chips was on the table in front of her. Alongside this was a bowl of what appeared to be apple crumble and custard. On the arm of the sofa was a chocolate bar. A large cardboard mug of Coke completed the meal.

"Martha! What on earth are you doing? We've spent ages sorting out your diet and you're eating all this! Do you know how much of my time has been spent working on helping you? You're supposed to be on a diet!" This was the only time I ever saw Joy really angry. Her voice wasn't raised, but there was no doubt she was very cross. I looked at Martha who just looked bemused and upset. I realised that this wasn't put on. She was genuinely bemused and incapable of understanding Joy's reaction.

"I'm doing everything you asked of me," she protested. "I always eat the diet you get sent in. Haven't eaten it yet, 'cos you said to eat it at one o'clock. I have my usual lunch at midday, then the diet meal at one. But your diet doesn't seem to be working, but I'm still trying".

This was another example of cross wiring in the communication. Martha truly believed that the special diet Joy had organised was an extra to her normal diet. She believed that it must contain some magical ingredient that would help her lose weight, despite continuing to consume her usual diet of burgers, chips and puddings. The sad fact was that Joy had failed to explain that the diet food, religiously delivered each day, at enormous expense, was not in addition to her other food, but was her total food. On seeing the special diet food, Martha had probably thought that this just couldn't be her total food for the day. It was too just too little and too green.

As we drove back to the surgery Joy, after being so cross, was now a peculiar mix of self-criticism and overflowing praise for me. She felt that she should have understood Martha's limited intelligence, and realised that she had failed to exactly define what was required of the special diet. It would all need to be documented and explained to Martha in a simpler and clearer form. At least the solution to the unanswered question of the weight gain had been solved. Joy believed she had me to thank. Rarely in my student nurse experience had I actually contributed anything of any real use to clinicians. This was a novelty not often replicated!

Back at the surgery Joy told me that she'd been left a message that Percy would be back next week. So trips with Joy were at an end. It was back to the crystal radios!

# CHAPTER THIRTY-ONE

Bonfire night. Bob was holding his yearly shindig at his home; a time to have the odd bevy, let off fireworks and have a bonfire of sorts. I attended aware that Bob's parties were planned only with regard to alcohol supplies. Other organisation, such as food and music, was haphazard. Bob's partner, Valerie, was a lovely and thoughtful woman, with a great sense of humour, but the impossible task of forcing Bob onto the straight and narrow, an area that he had always avoided, she was left to sort out the food, music and guest list.

Apart from tennis, Bob's had three main interests. His car, a terminally ill Humber, spent most of its time in the double garage with huge piles of machinery surrounding it. These car parts were partly removed from his Humber, but were added to with various scrap parts that Bob thought might come in useful "sometime". When the car worked, it was sedate and aristocratic. However, these times were rare. Bob didn't waste time in shops looking for car parts, but in scrap dealers. Always sure there was a cheaper way of fixing his precious car, it would remain in bits waiting for a particular rod or bolt which would land in Bob's hands at some stage in the future. Bob approached his car as he would a crossword, with thought and unhurriedness, even if it meant he was without transport for weeks. In reality he was rarely without a car. He used Valerie's and she walked.

His next interest was alcohol. It was the sheer money spent that staggered me. Bob was a scotch drinker, but he was also a drinker of gin, vodka, brandy or any spirit. He never had singles, but either doubles or quadruples. At lunchtime, or early evening, these were the chasers to his pints of beer. Drinking got in the way of his car, hence the slowness in fixing problems. If it was opening time Bob was usually there first. I once asked him if there was any drink he couldn't stomach.

He thought for some time. "Tomato juice."

"Why tomato juice?"

"I once got completely wrecked on Bloody Marys, so much so that I threw up everywhere. I've never touched a tomato juice since."

The third interest was the one that landed Bob in the most trouble. Women. Bob was round, small and balding, hardly a film star. No one thought of him as being a secure catch, let alone a good catch. Yet a succession of women threw themselves at him. Married and divorced, he was with his second partner, but only officially. Unofficially there were few women at the asylum that hadn't, at one time or another, been seduced by Bob. Despite this, ex-flames still flocked to him, so a party organised by Bob was a collection of females, most of whom were ex-mistresses, all of whom eyed each other with suspicion, but all of whom felt that Bob was magical. Most would restart the relationship if given enough of a chance. He was, of course, a complete scoundrel, but a scoundrel who genuinely brought more joy than sadness. Everyone broke into a smile when they saw him. He had that effect.

Bob asked me if I'd help him collect the alcohol from his local off-licence. He'd considered that doing his part of the purchasing was best done on his last days off prior to the party. Of course I'd help. Anything with him was an exhilarating experience.

The boxes surrounded the till. Bob paid the bill with his credit card. Wine, beer, vodka, gin, brandy. Everything in excess. The bill itself came to more than twice my weekly wages. Loading the car, then unloading it at his house, took two trips. Bob did another trip to collect fireworks, a small box of them. A token only! Although it was a bonfire party, Bob begrudged spending cash on non-alcoholic products.

Four days later I came across Bob in the Social Club. He'd dropped off the day report and was on "early doors", waiting in the Club for his shift to end. When he saw me, I was off duty, the rounds started. "By the way," he added after lining another scotch chaser to his first pint, "are you free tomorrow morning to help me with the booze purchasing?"

"But we did that a few days ago Bob."

"Yeah. But most of it's gone now. I don't like having too much booze in the house, so it's gone down a bit since then." Bob did polish off anything that was tempting. Parties like this were an expense that the International Monetary Fund would have difficulties with. A re-run of the trip to the off licence was required.

The party that weekend was in the kitchen, lounge and garden of Bob and Valerie's house in the city. The front of the house was really an extension of Bob's garage, bits of equipment, bits of cars, bits of ....he couldn't remember the significance of every piece of metal, but he was sure it would come in useful at some time. The only real indicator of a garden was a solitary pear tree Valerie had planted some years before. No pears had ever appeared, but they were still hopeful. "We could use them to make pear brandy," being Bob's comments on her arboreal development. Pears, to him, were only a useful commodity if used within an alcohol-based substance.

Inside on that night was a collection of people all with their own planned outcome for the Bonfire Night. None had come with significant expectations of the firework display. There were the ex-mistresses of Bob's. They were present to re-ignite Bob's desire for them. Then there was the male staff of the asylum, present to quaff the enormous quantities of alcohol before Bob did.

Among them was Niall, an early guest who'd come straight from his shift on Ward 2 and was now positioned in the kitchen on a beanbag. In the past Niall had been a prolific drinker, but with a liver that was giving up the ghost, a few drinks and he became incomprehensible, as well as prone to falls. A beanbag was usually available for him on the pretext that if embedded in this he couldn't get up, so couldn't fall. He slumped, blurry eyed, triple vodka clenched in his right hand, mumbling incoherently, but I was sure it was all swear words. He hadn't seen fireworks or bonfires for a decade or more. He was always too far gone to make the long trip out of the front door. People would pass him, mutter a greeting, get a refrain of gibberish in return and then move on. Intellectual discourse from Niall, at any stage of the evening after the first hour's drinking, was non-existent. I sat next to Niall, on a normal dining chair, to take over the duty of keeping his glass upright from Jack, who'd undertaken this task for the last hour. Jack talked quietly of the ending of his marriage, whilst Niall occasionally expressed expletives about anything around him, which we ignored. Jack was watching the ex-mistresses of Bob, eyeing up a potential short-term "bit of crumpet" for himself.

Mixed into this group of heavy asylum drinkers were a few social workers, friends of Valerie, gazing at the "cream" of psychiatric nurses as they tottered from a bit, to quite, to very drunk. Sometimes a short conversation between the nurses and social workers would start, but it was a brief chat before the to groups realised they had absolutely nothing in common. Niall didn't help the intermingling by waking with a start to hurl obscenities at the very words "social worker". In time the two groups would separate into different rooms, the social workers to the quiet of the lounge, with glasses of wine, the nurses to the kitchen area with the bulk of the alcohol.

"Come on out for the display!" shouted Bob. Jack and I left Niall, after removing his glass from him for the duration, to help with the bonfire and fireworks. Niall was alone with his thoughts, briefly, but then fell asleep.

The bonfire itself was really an excuse to be rid of rubbish collected over the past year: the cardboard boxes that held the booze, some sticks, a pillow or two, a couple of broken wooden shelving units, a St. Paul's Hospital counterpane, a broken deckchair with Hemsby written on the back, all topped off by a plastic doll with one leg, a bizarre "uni-dextered" Guy Fawkes.

Bob had been devouring the alcohol since lunchtime and his judgement was no longer good. Scrunching up some paper he pushed a few crumpled bits into the middle of the bonfire. Lighting the paper succeeded only in burning the paper. The wood, having been left in the garden, was wet. Ignition was not likely. More paper followed. Jack and I joined the paper scrunching exercise. No success.

"We need to get this bastard going before we start setting off the fireworks. Then I can get back to the booze. Oh, did you see that gorgeous woman in the kitchen. Not sure who she came with, but I'd like more time with her." Bob was now rushing. He disappeared into the garage, reappearing with a large plastic green petrol can.

"Stand back," he warned. Jack raised his eyebrows, then moved back. He was aware of Bob's impulsiveness with a bottle of scotch inside him. Everyone else now moved to a proper distance, apart from me. I stayed next to Bob, hoping to help with a simple matter of ignition. He poured some petrol hurriedly into a plastic mug and splashed this petrol towards the fire. A temporary whoosh, a sudden flash of ignited fuel, then back to a few flashes of flames.

Bob's assessment was that a small mug of petrol was insufficient. He removed the top of the petrol can and threw the can towards the fire. A sheet of flame tracked back towards the can, which caught fire brilliantly. The bonfire remained dim. With the can itself on fire it was only time before it would explode. Everyone rushed inside apart from Jack and me. Giving it a glimpse, assessing its danger, Bob threw the whole flaming can away from himself, shouting a warning to others to stay away. They had already gone.

In his haste to be rid of the flaming can, Bob had failed to check where it landed. The can came to rest against the thin trunk of the pear tree. It was here that it exploded. The pear tree burned rather well, lasting long after the bonfire had gone out. "Well, it never gave us any fucking pears anyway," was Bob's simple summing up of the situation.

He decided to save the fireworks for next year. Everyone had already decided it was much safer inside anyway.

Years later the charred stump of the pear tree reminded me of that night. It was probably a Bonfire Night that Guy Fawkes would have approved of.

# CHAPTER THIRTY-TWO

Christmas. A time of good cheer but a very dangerous time in mental health. The pressures, the forced family gatherings, the hype, all lead to a lethal combination that can trigger the unexpected. I hate Christmas.

I was coming to an end, not just of my community experience but also of my training. I was beginning to think about where I should apply for a permanent job, in what sphere I wanted to work and my exams.

Christmas was around the corner and this was my first Christmas since starting as a student nurse that I wasn't working. I was to finish on Christmas Eve, before driving home to my family on Christmas Day, just in time for the champagne and present opening. I would then have a week's work before New Year. Then back into the School of Nursing for final studies leading to the exams.

That last week was a time to tie up loose ends, in theory. In practice it was a chance to relax, play some indoor tennis, get down the Social Club, drink ale. Meeting up with Jack and Bob we arranged tennis for the New Year. However, as well as that, Jack invited me to join Ward 7 for their Christmas Party, a Christmas Eve afternoon "bash" for patients, relatives and staff. Perhaps accepting that I could be the butt for the retelling of the "toffee mousse story", but also because Ward 7 was the ward I had enjoyed most, the invite was welcome. I was pleased and grateful to be included. The Ward 7 party always led to a heavy drinking session at the Social Club, so it was an invite from three o'clock in the afternoon to midnight.

That last Christmas Eve was my day for study, as well as visiting Percy. It was a Friday. I was due to visit Percy at midday, the same time every Friday. I knew that Joy would be visiting Percy on that Christmas Eve morning. I thought about the party that afternoon on Ward 7. I'd be back in the Nurses Home the day after Boxing Day, bored by then of the good will! No one would be planning to see Percy that week; Joy would be away, Deb would be off – probably discussing car mechanics with her sons. Perhaps, instead of visiting Percy today, it would be better to organise a visit next week. Joy was seeing him today anyway. That would solve both today for me, and next week for Percy. Feeling quite pleased with myself for this simple solution I phoned Joy.

"Joy. Hi it's Stuart here."

"Hi Stuart, Happy Christmas to you. What can I do for you?"

"You know there's this party on Ward 7 today. I'm due to see Percy today at midday, but neither you nor Deb plan to see him next week. I thought it might be a good scheme for me to see him next week instead of today. I've nothing to do then, Percy will be bored. He'll get a visit this week from you and next week from me. What'd you think?"

"OK. I'm seeing him after my next patient and I'll tell him then. Sounds good to me. Give Jack and Ward 12 my love. See you in the New Year."

The phone call ended, I returned to working my books, preparing for finals. Radio 2 was providing me with background music as I sat in my room in the Nurses Home. It was all Christmassy music to get me, and everyone else, in the mood. It didn't. As I listened the 11 o'clock news came on. I had only one ear cocked. Unfortunately it wasn't cocked enough. The news was nothing to focus on, but I was just aware of a minor item of news, well down the running order. The Newsreader announced, "it's being suggested that parts of British Aerospace may be sold off in order to begin privatisation of some public sector companies." I heard it, but didn't absorb it.

I left for Ward 7, the Honda 70 now filled with petrol for the journey home tomorrow. Jack was on duty, preparing for the party. I helped with the toilet round before lunch, helping myself to a small beer between trips to the "hooking on" procedures. Barbara arrived, going through the blood results that had come in, blocking the space in the cramped office.

On my third run to the toilets, most of the patients now sitting up at the dining tables, Barbara called me. There was a phone call. I reached over the hatch to take the call.

"Hi, Stuart, it's Joy here."

"Hiya. Can't you leave me alone?" I asked sarcastically.

"Sorry Stuart. I've just come back from Percy. He's on a real downer. Did you hear the news?"

"No, what news?"

"About the privatisation of parts of British Aerospace."

"Oh, yeah, just heard it. So what?"

"But that Percy's firm. He's devastated."

"Christ! It just rang a bell when I heard it. But I never connected it."

"I've never seen him so angry and cross," she continued. "He was in tears telling me about it. I told him not to worry, but he sees it as a personal blow. I then told him about you coming to see him next week, instead of this."

"Was he happy with that? Did it perk him up?" I asked, thinking that at least he'd have someone to rant to next week.

"No. Sorry. It didn't. Just made him even worse. He said that you'd told him you'd come today, as you always do, but he said that as you obviously felt that other things were more important, then don't bother coming back. He doesn't want you back again. He's in quite a strop"

"Shit. I thought he'd like that change. Sorry Joy. I'll come straight over now. I'll try to get him to talk to me. I'll apologise. I thought he'd think it was a good idea. I'm on my way. Will you be at the surgery?"

"Yeah. I'll be there." With that the call ended.

Barbara and Jack were both with me now, overhearing the end of the call.

Barbara was first to chip in. "I've seen him like this on too many occasions. He'll take to his bed. You'll need to get him in. Don't mess around. He'll be fine here. We'll make sure he has a Christmas present and we'll feed him up on turkey."

Jack confirmed he'd got a free bed but, as this was in the main dormitory, he'd move a patient from a side room so that Percy could go in there. Both encouraged haste to get to Percy's place.

The Honda screamed as I drove to get to Percy's bungalow. Pulling off my helmet I knocked on the front door. No answer. I knocked louder. Still no answer. I went round the back, knocking even louder on the back door. No good.

Back at the surgery I spoke to Joy. "Is this the usual?" I asked.

"Yeah. He'll have gone to bed again. He just can't take the pressure of changes."

"You mean the sale of British Aerospace?"

"Both that and you not seeing him today."

I'd made a terrible error in changing my visit. What could I do now?

"Thank God," said Joy, "that we got this duplicate key made for his front door. You'll get in there. I'll come with you, if you want."

"Thanks."

Joy took the key as we crossed the road to the bungalow. Outside the front door Joy inserted the key into the lock. "I can't turn it. It just won't turn at all," Joy said, showing frustration.

I pushed her out of the way. I jiggled the key trying to get it to turn. I was no more successful than Joy. The key would go in but not turn. Why? It did last time we used it. I looked at the key, tried again, still no success. We both went round the back. Knocking on the bedroom window Joy shouted at Percy. "Open up Percy, we're getting cold out here. We want to have a chat to see how you are, that's all."

No answer. We stood and looked at each other. Joy asked me what to do. I was already stumped. Solutions were not forthcoming. "I'll phone Jack and Barbara on the ward."

Back at the surgery I contacted Barbara, telling her the situation. Barbara only confirmed my bafflement. "Deb told me about the key. I can't understand why it won't work."

"What shall I do?"

"He'll need to come in. If there's no way he'll let you in, get the police out and break down the back door. Then look after him until the ambulance arrives. I'll arrange the ambulance. You and Joy arrange the police."

Joy and I leant against the porch pillars of the surgery, awaiting the police. Joy knew someone at the local station, so they were coming as well. Both of us stood in silence, pondering, ruminating about Percy. At last we saw the flashing lights of the panda car approach. At Joy's request, no siren sounded. Percy wouldn't appreciate this.

Joy introduced me to the officer she knew. We were just out of sight of the bungalow.

In my long experience in psychiatry the police have always acted with superb professionalism when it comes to mental health issues. Their usual answer to any question "What do you want from us?" They then followed this.

"I need to get in there," I told the uniformed officer. "He'll be in the bedroom, covered with a continental quilt. I need to get him to Ward 12. So I need entry to the house. Once you get me in, disappear fast. Percy won't want anything to do with you."

"No prob."

We walked round the back, me still tapping on windows, shouting to Percy that I wanted to talk to him. At the back door the officer asked if I really wanted him to break in. I confirmed it. "But when the door gives, you move back, out of the way. Percy doesn't like the police."

A Yale lock held the door. The officer turned, braced and then kicked the door. The doorjamb split easily. The door swung open, smashing the kitchen surface at full stretch.

I had never seen Percy smile. He just didn't smile. So it was the briefest sense of difference that hit me first. Facing me, he was taller. He was at my height. How odd. But the smile wasn't really a smile. It was a grimace. Mouth slightly open, dribble hanging from his lower lip, Percy still swung gently on the rope, the draught of the door passing his nose had probably caused this slight movement. Only inches from the floor, his feet pointed downwards. Blood drained from my face, probably mirroring the grey face of Percy. Christmas Eve had suddenly lost all its appeal.

I backed off. The police officer went in first, grabbing his waist to lift him, taking the strain off the rope. I climbed onto the work surface. The rope had been threaded carefully through a hole in the ceiling, made by the removal of a ceiling tile, and then looped over a joist. Without the weight of Percy I found the knot easy to unravel. We laid Percy on the floor of his kitchen. He was becoming stiff. He was very dead.

Joy, wordless, stepped carefully over the body to the front door. I followed. We both were checking the same thing. Why hadn't the door opened, half an hour ago? We looked at the front door. We both saw it at the same time. I called the police officer, checking that I could pry in this way, not wanting to further blemish my actions.

"Can I get this out?"

"Yeah," he replied. "Its not a crime scene."

I worked the nail loose, removing it from the latch. Percy, at some point in time, had carefully drilled a hole through the latch. This allowed him to insert a nail preventing its retraction, hence why we were unable to gain access. Percy had obviously planned that if, and when, he wanted to end it all, he would have both the equipment and the privacy to implement his terrible legacy. The safety system of the extra key, which he'd agreed to, was a sop to us. He had ensured it would make no difference.

As we were inspecting the latch, the ambulance arrived. Seeing the outcome, they requested the local doctor to attend. It was now all procedure. Joy and I left, back to her office, to the telephone, for the phone call to Ward 7. Speaking to Jack I confirmed what had occurred, with him promising to inform Barbara and Deb. With no known relatives there was nothing else to do. I returned to Ward 7, to a Christmas Party that had just been turned into a wake.

There are, I think, certain points in life that become life changers. This was my first professional life changer. My activities and decisions on that Christmas Eve were something that I analysed through all the next year. From that analysis I think I became a better nurse. However, the lesson learned that day was a very expensive one.

A life, not necessarily an exciting one, had ended, due to circumstances of overlooked fate. I had, at least partially, triggered the termination of Percy's existence, at his own hand, by my lack of focus, my lack of thoughtfulness, my lack of understanding psychological trauma. A better nurse, or perhaps just a better person, would have realised the dangers in working with Percy. I had failed to notice the warning signs, indeed, had contributed to the pain, so that due to both my actions and inactions Percy was now cold on a slab in some mortuary. I had thought of my interactions with him as being easy compared to the volatility and frank mental illness I had seen in so many others. I was wrong.

The quiet man in the bungalow caused greater pain than all the rest put together.

As I reflect I am still startled by the response of people after that event. The Ward 7 staff all came to give me a hug. They all impressed on me the long-term psychological pain of Percy, sometimes backing it up with, "he was bound to do it sometime." The sympathy should have been transposed into a huge kick up the arse. I knew that my actions fell far short that morning. I had failed to pick up on the privatisation of British Aerospace. I had passed messages through Joy to Percy, rather than discussing changes with him directly. I had altered the vital routines that Percy came to rely on. I had convinced myself that these changes to the fixed schedule were for Percy's benefit, when in fact, they were for my benefit. Lastly, I had sought to make these changes for good intentions. I had just found out what the road to hell was paved with.

I learned so much from this episode. From that time on I never presumed what was best for someone else. I assessed before action. Yet the main change after Percy was that I now began to think about, to really think about, the fragility of people in psychological distress. Psychological pain is just as real as physical pain. But it was just such a shame that Percy's suspended corpse was the detonator required to explode this bombshell over me.

After more than three years in the asylum, of the disturbed, the angry, the tearful and the weird, I had, as far as I was concerned, failed my finals in that last patient related action.

Within weeks I had actually passed my finals, being granted the letters R.M.N. after my name. I was to be let loose on the unwary. I now had to demonstrate that Percy's hard lesson could make a safe, practicing mental health nurse.

Grace, with the lovely head of white flowing locks, and Percy, the gentle man, the crystal radio buff, had provided me with my hardest, yet my most important, lessons. Two lives wrecked. I could only hope that I could repay them by being a nurse that could also change lives for the better.

It was the start of my professional career.

# ABOUT THE AUTHOR

**Stuart Townsend** is a pen name. Stuart read Theology at Cardiff University before embarking on a career in Psychiatric Nursing. From 1981, as a qualified nurse, he worked in all areas of psychiatry, before specializing in elderly psychiatry and then community psychiatry,
both in the United Kingdom and New Zealand.
During his entire career he worked as a clinical nurse, having professional contact with people in distress and mental anguish in the front line of psychiatric nursing.
He retired from clinical work in 2010, to concentrate on writing and training.
Stuart is married to a psychiatric nurse specializing in forensic psychiatry. They have three sons. His interests include history, golf and bridge.

He lives in Nottinghamshire U.K.

Printed in Great Britain
by Amazon